We are honored to present this
valuable book on kibbud av va'eim
to the distinguished mechanchim at the
5785/2024 Torah Umesorah convention

In memory of our dear parents

בראנדל בת ר' משה דוד

ר' יעקב אליעזר בן ר' יצחק הלוי

ר' יעקב שלמה בן ר' יחיאל

Rabbi Yaakov Pressman —
a "rebbi's rebbi"

May the inspiration gained from this book
be a zechus for their neshamos.

ArtScroll® Series

Rabbi Nosson Scherman / Rabbi Gedaliah Zlotowitz

General Editors

Rabbi Meir Zlotowitz ז״ל, *Founder*

THE JACOB ROTH EDITION

My Parents

Published by

ARTSCROLL
Mesorah Publications, ltd

and Me

HEARTWARMING STORIES *for teens*

RABBI SHIMON FINKELMAN

SPECIAL SECTION: HALACHOS OF KIBBUD AV V'EIM

FIRST EDITION
First Impression ... August 2022
Second Impression ... October 2024

Published and Distributed by
MESORAH PUBLICATIONS, LTD.
313 Regina Avenue / Rahway, N.J. 07065

Distributed in Europe by
LEHMANNS
Unit E, Viking Business Park
Rolling Mill Road
Jarrow, Tyne & Wear NE32 3DP
England

Distributed in Australia & New Zealand by
GOLDS WORLD OF JUDAICA
3-13 William Street
Balaclava, Melbourne 3183
Victoria Australia

Distributed in Israel by
SIFRIATI / A. GITLER — BOOKS
POB 2351
Bnei Brak 51122

Distributed in South Africa by
KOLLEL BOOKSHOP
Northfield Centre, 17 Northfield Avenue
Glenhazel 2192, Johannesburg, South Africa

ARTSCROLL® SERIES
MY PARENTS AND ME

ITEM CODE: MYMH
ISBN 10: 1-4226-3228-8
ISBN 13: 978-1-4226-3228-4

Typography by CompuScribe at ArtScroll Studios, Ltd.
Printed in the United States of America.
Bound by Sefercraft, Quality Bookbinders, Ltd., Rahway NJ

My Parents and Me is dedicated in loving memory of

Jacob Roth ע״ה

יעקב אפרים ע״ה בן יבלח״ט ר׳ טובי׳ הענוך נ״י

During his twenty-four years of life in this world, Jacob was a devoted son, wonderful brother and uncle, and good friend to all who knew him. He was kind and caring. With a warm smile and words of encouragement, he was always there for those who needed him.

He learned about *kibbud av va'eim* from his teachers, but he lived *kibbud av va'eim* far beyond what he was taught, and his sterling *middos* were an example to all.

When he tended to his own needs, he still remembered ours. Jacob was easy to talk to. He'd give us advice, cheer us up when we needed it, and share our life's joys with us.

It's impossible to describe all of Jacob's beautiful *middos* in just a few words. With that being said, simply put, he was a wonderful son.

My Parents and Me is a most fitting tribute to Jacob's memory.

It is our hope that this book touches the hearts and minds of all those who learn from it. May they develop fine *middos*, and may that inspiration be a merit for Jacob in *Shamayim*.

Dedicated by his loving parents

Theodore and Rhonda Roth
and Family

בס"ד

שמואל קמנצקי
Rabbi S. Kamenetsky

2018 Upland Way
Philadelphia, PA 19131

Home: 215-473-2798
Study: 215-473-1212

בס"ד, י"ט סיון תשע"ט

כבוד ידידי מרביץ תורה לעדרים הרה"ג רבי שמעון הכהן פינקעלמאן שליט"א, ואתו עמו, כהנא מסייע כהנא, הרה"ג ר' זכרי' הכהן וואלערשטיין שליט"א,

קבלתי העלים לדוגמא מהספר על עניני כיבוד אב ואם שבדעתכם להוציא לאור בקרוב, והוא אוצר בלום הרבה רעיונות, עובדות והנהגות, וגם כמה הלכות למעשה הנוגעים לענין כיבוד אב ואם. ניכר בהספר כמה עמל ויגיעה ומחשבה הושקע בו כדי להוציא מתח"י דבר המתוקן, והוא דבר השוה לכל נפש שכל מי שיעיין בו ימצא מה שלבו חפץ.

מובטחני שכל מי שילמוד בספר זה ימצא בו דברי חפץ, והספר יביא תועלת לבחורים ולכל מי שרוצה לחזק עצמו במצוה חשובה הלזו.

ברכתי שיזכו להמשיך בעבודתם להפיץ תורה ולזכות את הרבים עד ביאת גואל צדק.

שמואל קמנצקי

This michtav berachah and the ones that follow appear in Honor Them Revere Them, which the author wrote in collaboration with Rabbi Zechariah Wallerstein z"l.

בס"ד

משה וואלפסאן
משגיח רוחני, ישיבה תורה ודעת
ורב דביהמ"ד אמונת ישראל

Rabbi Moshe Wolfson
1574 43rd Street
Brooklyn, New York 11219

ב"ה כ"ה סיון תש"פ

ידידי יקירי מאד נעלה הרה"ג ר' שמעון פינקעלמאן שליט"א זכו לי' מן השמים להיות מרביץ תורה לעדרים ולחנך תלמידים הרבה לתורה ויראת שמים וכל מדה נכונה. אמנם קים בנפשי' עצת קהלת "ויותר מהמה בני הזהר עשות ספרים הרבה" וכבר זכה שספריו הנחמדים והמלאים ומפיקים יראת שמים, נתפרסמו ונעשו נחלת הכלל וחוגים בהם עשרות אלפים מאחינו בני ישראל המוצאים בהם נחת.

ועתה מוציא לאור, יחד עם הרב זכרי' וואלערשטיין שליט"א, ספר נפלא, ותבניתו הוא ללמוד כל יום מימות השנה לימוד וסיפור בענין כבוד אב ואם שהיא מיסודות תורתנו הקדושה, ונכתב ומסודר בטוב טעם ודעת, ומובטחני בעזהי"ת שיהי' לתועלת גדול לכל ההוגים בו, וירגישו בו טובה גדולה בנפש.

והנני לברכו שיזכה עוד ועוד שיפוצו מעינותיו חוצה לנחת רוח לבורא ית"ש ולנחת רוח לעמו ישראל, ויזכה להצלחה וברכה, ימלא השי"ת כל משאלותיו לטובה.

בעוז ידידות
משה וואלפסאן

בס"ד

YESHIVA DARCHEI TORAH 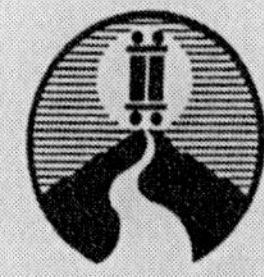 ישיבה דרכי תורה

YAAKOV & ILANA MELOHN CAMPUS, IN MEMORY OF REB YOSEF MELOHN, ז"ל

הרב יעקב בנדר
ראש הישיבה

Tammuz 5779

לכבוד ידידי הרה"ג המופלא, מרביץ תורה
ב[illegible], ר' שמעון פינקלמאן שליט"א
וגם ידידי עושה חסד לאלפים, [illegible]
הרה"ר ר' זכרי' וואלערשטיין שליט"א

I have had the zechus of working with Rabbi Shimon Finkelman for many years. We are privileged to have Reb Shimon as a rebbe in our yeshiva. He brings the old-time ruchniyus, yet he is able to connect with the American crowd through his ehrlichkeit, responsibility, caring, and achrayus.

Kibud Av V'aim was a number-one priority in the home in which Rabbi Finkelman was raised. Rabbi Finkelman's parents raised children who are all outstanding members of the Torah world today, extraordinary mentschen, who would jump into the fire for their parents and for any Yid.

This sefer explains the mitzvah of Kibud Av V'aim and is essential for every Jewish home. I would even suggest that every family learn from this sefer for five minutes every Shabbos. This is written by an individual who truly understands every aspect of Kibud Av V'aim.

A debt of gratitude is also due Rabbi Zechariah Wallerstein, who spearheaded this project and worked with Rabbi Finkelman to produce this magnificent work.

May Reb Shimon be a marbitz Torah for Yeshiva Darchei Torah and for all of Klal Yisroel for many years to come.

בכבוד גדול וידידות עוז!
יעקב בנדר

MESIVTA CHAIM SHLOMO • BEIS MEDRASH HEICHAL DOVID • KOLLEL AVREICHIM • RABENSTEIN LEARNING CENTER
257 Beach 17th Street, Far Rockaway, NY 11691 • Tel: 718-868-2300 Ext. 217 • Fax: 718-868-4690

YISROEL REISMAN | **ישראל רייזמאן**
1460 EAST 19TH STREET | **ישיבה תורה ודעת**
BROOKLYN, NY, 11230 | **אגודת ישראל בפלאטבוש**

בס״ד

תמוז תשע״ט

The mitzvah of *kibbud av va'eim* seems simple enough. After all, the concept of respecting one's elders is a universal value. It seems like a logical mitzvah. While its observance requires self control, the rules would seem to require little study time.

Approximately thirty years ago, we were learning *Masechta Kiddushin* in yeshivah and our studies brought us to the *sugya* of *kibbud av va'eim*.

In his *Dibros Moshe* (*ha'arah* 14), Rav Moshe Feinstein *zt"l* makes the following statement:

Kibbud av va'eim requires that a child show honor by taking care of his parents' needs. There are also specific requirements regarding *morah av va'eim*, revering one's parents. Nevertheless, if a parents tells a child to do something which does not pertain to the parent's comfort or honor, Rav Moshe argues that the child is not obligated to obey. This might include the common parental request to "Put on a sweater" or "Eat your vegetables."

When I discussed this with my rebbi, Rav Avraham Pam zt"l, he took serious exception to Rav Moshe's ruling. He cited a *Maharal* in *Parshas Yisro* that would indicate the reverse. After some research, I defended Rav Moshe by pointing to the *Sefer Yerei'im* which seems to support Rav Moshe's opinion. For a week or two we continued the discussion, finding additional indications one way or the other, ultimately coming to the conclusion that this may depend on the understanding of a *Rashba* in *Yevamos* 4b, and the *Gra's* citing of the *Rashba* in his notes to *Yoreh Deah*.

Ultimately, Rav Pam's opinion took the form of a section in his *Sefer Atarah LaMelech*.

On reflection, I was struck by this discussion. Here, we have a common example of the mitzvah of *kibbud av va'eim* and two contemporary *gedolim* disagree over its parameters. Clearly, the observance of *kibbud av va'eim* is not simply keeping to the instinctive feeling of honoring elders. Rather, as with all mitzvos, it is an obligation which we must pursue by studying the mitzvah and its very specific aspects as they are taught to us by *Chazal*.

We express our thanks to Rabbi Shimon Finkelman and Rabbi Zechariah Wallerstein for producing a *sefer* that is a key to fulfilling this mitzvah. As we study the mitzvah, we realize that it requires even more study. The particulars of *Torah she'Baal Peh* are eye opening and cause us to reflect and rededicate ourselves to this all important mitzvah.

May this extraordinary opportunity to study this mitzvah daily spawn a new awakening regarding the mitzvah which *Talmud Yerushalmi* calls, *"chamura shebachamuros*."

קהילת שער שמים

71 East Willow Road
Spring Valley, N.Y. 10977
הרב יוסף ויינר — מרא ד'אתרא

בס"ד
תמוז תשע"ט

Kibbud av va'eim is a foundation of Jewish life, which is why it is one of the *Aseres HaDibros*. In my own *kehillah,* I have devoted well over a year of nightly *shiurim* to this very crucial topic.

Over the past half year, Rabbi Shimon Finkelman has been sending me the manuscript of this book, chapter by chapter, for my perusal and comments. Rabbi Finkelman, in collaboration with Rabbi Zechariah Wallerstein, has done the *frum* community a tremendous service by producing a book on *kibbud av va'eim* which is highly readable and highly informative. It can be read and appreciated by a sixteen year old and a sixty year old.

The book is a masterful mix of practical *halachah*, *hashkafah* and stories. I am certain that anyone who reads it will be inspired to raise their level of *kibbud av va'eim*. And if their parents are no longer in this world, they will be inspired to do more for their *neshamos* than they had done previously.

May the authors continue to be *marbeh kvod Shamayim* and be *mezakeh es harabim*.

בברכת התורה,
יוסף ויינר

תְּפִלַּת הַיְלָדִים עַל הוֹרֵיהֶם

(מסידור ישועות ישראל מבעל מסגרת השולחן)

יְהִי רָצוֹן מִלְּפָנֶיךָ ה׳ אֱלֹקֵינוּ וֵאלֹקֵי אֲבוֹתֵינוּ שֶׁיִּהְיוּ אָבִינוּ וְאִמֵּנוּ וַאֲנַחְנוּ בְּרִיאִים וַחֲזָקִים לַעֲבֹד אוֹתְךָ בֶּאֱמֶת. וְתַשְׁפִּיעַ לָהֶם וְלָנוּ פַּרְנָסָה בְּרֶוַח וְהַצְלָחָה מְרֻבָּה וְכָל טוּב לַעֲבֹד אוֹתְךָ בֶּאֱמֶת וּבְשִׂמְחָה. וְתֵן בְּלִבֵּנוּ לִשְׁמֹעַ בְּקוֹל אָבִינוּ וְאִמֵּנוּ וְהוֹשִׁיעֵנוּ שֶׁנְּכַבֵּד אוֹתָם תָּמִיד כַּאֲשֶׁר רְצוֹנְךָ הַטּוֹב עִמָּנוּ וְנַעֲבֹד אוֹתְךָ בֶּאֱמֶת. וִיגַדְּלוּ אָבִינוּ וְאִמֵּנוּ אוֹתָנוּ לְתוֹרָה וּלְחֻפָּה וּלְמַעֲשִׂים טוֹבִים. וְיִהְיוּ מֻצְלָחִים בִּבְרִיאוּת וְכָל טוּב וַעֲשִׁירוּת לִתֵּן לָנוּ מֹהַר וּמַתָּן וְכָל טוּב בְּסֵבֶר פָּנִים יָפוֹת. וּמַלֵּא כָּל מִשְׁאֲלוֹת לְבָבֵנוּ לְטוֹבָה. אָבִינוּ שֶׁבַּשָּׁמַיִם הוֹשִׁיעֵנוּ כָּל זֶה בִּכְלַל כָּל יִשְׂרָאֵל. וְנִזְכֶּה לְהַגְדִּיל כְּבוֹד שִׁמְךָ הַגָּדוֹל וּכְבוֹד תּוֹרָתְךָ תָּמִיד.

יִהְיוּ לְרָצוֹן אִמְרֵי פִי וְהֶגְיוֹן לִבִּי לְפָנֶיךָ ה׳ צוּרִי וְגֹאֲלִי.

A Tefillah for Children on Behalf of Their Parents

(from Siddur Yeshuos Yisrael by the author of Misgeres HaShulchan)

May it be Your will, Hashem, our G-d, and the G-d of our forefathers, that our father, our mother, and ourselves should be healthy and strong so that we can serve You in truth. Grant them and ourselves abundant sustenance, much success, and all that is good, so that we can serve You in truth and in joy. Instill in our hearts the desire to want to obey our father and mother; and help us to honor them always, as is Your good desire, and may we serve You in truth. May our father and mother merit to raise us to [a life of] Torah, the marriage canopy, and good deeds. May they be healthy and successful, and be blessed with much bounty and wealth, so that they can grant us our marriage necessities and all that is good with a cheerful countenance. Fulfill all of our heartfelt requests for the good.

Our Father in Heaven: Help us with all of the above together with the entire Jewish people. May we merit to enhance the honor of Your Name and the honor of Your Torah, always.

May the expressions of my mouth and the thoughts of my heart find favor before You, Hashem, my Rock and my Redeemer.

Dedicated in memory of

Rabbi Zechariah Wallerstein z"l

הרב זכריה שמעון בן ר׳ יצחק הכהן ז״ל

founder of Ohr Naava and other groundbreaking initiatives.
His caring and vision changed the lives of thousands. He was the driving force behind the publication of *Honor Them Revere Them*.
May he be a *meilitz yosher* for his distinguished family,
his scores of *talmidim* and *talmidos*, and all of Klal Yisrael.

Table of Contents

Part I: Stories

Part 2: Halachos

Introduction

A little over two years ago, ArtScroll/Mesorah published *Honor Them, Revere Them — A Lesson a Day on Kibbud Av VaEim,* which I was privileged to write, in collaboration with Rabbi Zechariah Wallerstein *z"l.* A few months later, I was contacted by someone who wants to remain anonymous. He told me:

> *Every summer, a man comes around my neighborhood selling sefarim and books. I usually buy something, and I've found that Hashem helps me choose something that ends up being very useful.*
>
> *This past summer, I chose a new book, "Honor Them, Revere Them." I bought it because I've been living with guilt since the sudden passing of my father many years ago when I was relatively young. I felt that my kibbud av toward him had been lacking; in fact, I went to his kever (grave) to ask mechilah. It's not that I'd been disrespectful toward him — that was certainly not the case. But I'd never gone out of my way to do anything for him, especially after I left for the dormitory and later married.*
>
> *After my father's passing, I told myself that I wouldn't make the same mistake with my mother. From now on, I resolved, my kibbud eim would be different.*
>
> *But it wasn't. I still called my mother only once a week, on Friday, to wish her a good Shabbos. I came with my family for Shabbos once in a while. Nothing special.*

So I bought this book. And I promptly put it away to be used at some later date.

Then Elul came, the month when we start preparing ourselves for Rosh Hashanah. I felt that it was time to accept upon myself something new. So I took this new book about kibbud av va'eim off the shelf and began to read — a lesson a day, every day.

After about forty days, the lessons were seeping into my bones. And I knew that now was the time to make a significant change in my relationship with my mother.

It was now or never.

I began to call my mother every night. It was uncomfortable at first, but the more I saw how much she appreciated it, the easier it became. My mother wanted to talk, and I learned to be a good listener. Our entire relationship changed.

I am so grateful that I have a mother whom I can honor and love, and whose life I can brighten by being a good son.

Kibbud av va'eim is one of the most important mitzvos in the Torah. That's why it's in the *Aseres HaDibros,* the Ten Commandments. We honor our parents out of gratitude for all that they do for us from the moment we're born. Another important reason why we must honor them is that they are the ones Hashem chose to bring our *neshamos* down to this world. They are "partners with Hashem" in our creation. That's why the Gemara (*Kiddushin* 30b) says that when we honor our parents, it's like we are honoring Hashem.

When our ancestors were in the *Midbar,* parents did not have to do very much for their children. Their food, the *mahn,* came from Heaven. Their water came from the Well of Miriam. Their clothing grew with them and never wore out. Still, children had to honor their parents, because they were Hashem's partners in their birth.

Family life is found only among human beings. Animals don't

remain attached for life to their parents, but humans do. Why did Hashem make people this way? Rabbi Samson Raphael Hirsch explains that Judaism could not exist without family life. Children, parents, grandparents, great-grandparents, and so on are part of an unbroken chain stretching back to Har Sinai. Fathers and mothers teach their children how to make a *berachah,* how to say *Shema.* At the Seder, parents and grandparents teach their children and grandchildren about *Yetzias Mitzrayim,* and a lot more about our glorious history.

Our parents care for us both physically and spiritually.

Different Levels

As we saw in the story above, there are many levels of *kibbud av va'eim.* At first, that young man called his mother only once a week. Later, he spoke with her every night and even went out of his way to make her life more enjoyable. (See the story "Time Well Spent" in this volume.)

Sometimes, well-meaning people can make terrible mistakes in how they act toward their parents.

> *A young man in Yerushalayim whom we'll call Naftali was making a Shabbos bris for his newborn. As Naftali and his parents were on their way to the bris, they met the gaon Rabbi Shlomo Zalman Auerbach. Naftali took the opportunity to ask for a berachah for his new baby.*
>
> *But Rav Shlomo Zalman seemed taken aback by what he saw: The baby's grandparents were each carrying several bags of things for the bris and the kiddush that would follow, while the baby's father was not carrying anything at all.*
>
> *Realizing what was troubling Rav Shlomo Zalman, Naftali explained, "I'm machmir (very strict with myself) not to use the eruv, even though it's kosher [so I couldn't carry anything], but my parents use the eruv. That's why they're carrying and I'm not."*

Rav Shlomo Zalman was very upset. If the eruv was kosher and halachah permitted carrying, how could Naftali let his parents carry all those packages while he carried nothing? Respect for parents is commanded by the Torah. Naftali's conduct was a non-halachic stringency. Was that proper respect for his father and mother? Certainly not!

A few nights later, Rav Shlomo Zalman delivered a shmuess at Yeshivah Kol Torah, where he was the Rosh Yeshivah. Without mentioning Naftali's name, he devoted his entire shmuess to this incident, using it as an example of how a person can mistakenly think he is doing something very good when in fact he is doing something very wrong.

Tzaddikim such as the Chazon Ish and the Manchester Rosh Yeshivah (Rabbi Yehudah Zev Segal) would tell *yeshivah bachurim* who were heading home for Yom Tov: "Before you leave yeshivah, review the halachos of *kibbud av va'eim.*" Every *ben Torah* and *bas Yisrael* wants to show proper respect for his or her parents. Sometimes, though, we make mistakes without thinking. Learning the halachos about *kibbud av va'eim* not only gives us knowledge, it also reminds us to be careful about how we observe this mitzvah.

That is the purpose of this book. Its more than one hundred stories are examples of proper and even exceptional *kibbud av va'eim.* And the halachos in the second section give us the basics of what a child should and should not do when interacting with parents.

We hope that you'll enjoy this book. When you finish it, put it on an accessible shelf and read it again in a few months. This will give you an awareness that will help you do the great mitzvah of *kibbud av va'eim* in a way that will bring *nachas* to Hashem and to your parents, and will bring *berachah* to you and your future generations.

Acknowledgments

My Parents and Me is to a large degree adapted from *Honor Them, Revere Them.* Rabbi Zechariah Wallerstein *z"l,* a man of great vision and passion, saw a need for a lesson-a-day book on these laws. He suggested that we collaborate on such a book. I am eternally grateful to Rabbi Wallerstein for that, and for inviting me to collaborate on our previous book, *Let There be Rain,* a lesson-a-day on *hakaras hatov,* feeling and displaying gratitude.

His passing is a tremendous loss for *Klal Yisrael.* May Hashem comfort his distinguished family, and his thousands of *talmidim* and *talmidos.* And may he be a *meilitz yosher* for them, to bring even greater *siyata diShmaya* to Ohr Naava and the other important projects he created and developed.

I am deeply grateful to Rabbi Yosef Viener, Rav of Kehilas Shaar HaShamayim in Spring Valley, for reviewing the Halachos section of this book and making important comments. Rabbi Viener also reviewed *Honor Them, Revere Them* in its entirety. For that, too, I am grateful.

My Parents and Me is the result of a phone conversation I had about a year ago with ArtScroll/Mesorah's very creative President and co-General Editor, Rabbi Gedaliah Zlotowitz. When I mentioned to Reb Gedaliah that a yeshivah rebbi was inspiring his *talmidim* with stories from *Honor Them, Revere Them,* he immediately suggested that we create the kind of book that you now hold in your hands.

I am grateful to Reb Gedaliah for his friendship and for his readiness to help me in any way that he can. And I am forever indebted to his unforgettable father, Rabbi Meir Zlotowitz *z"l*, one of the great visionaries and *marbitzei Torah* of our generation, for allowing me to be part of the ArtScroll family and for all that he did for me over the years.

Rabbi Nosson Scherman is one of *Klal Yisrael's* great treasures. I am very fortunate to have Rabbi Scherman as my rebbi, guide, and mentor. He is never too busy to give me his time and sage advice, whenever I reach out to him. May Hashem grant him many more years in good health to spread the light of Torah in this world.

The beautiful graphics design of this book is thanks to the input of the master artist Rabbi Sheah Brander, whose talent has enhanced *kevod haTorah* through ArtScroll's thousands of books and *sefarim*. May he continue *l'hagdil Torah ul'hadirah* for many years to come.

My thanks to my *yedid* Rabbi Avrohom Biderman, who is always ready to assist me whenever I call on him. Thank you to Reb Mendy Herzberg for coordinating the production of this book with his usual patience and pleasantness. My appreciation to Reb Eli Kroen for lending his expertise to the graphics design.

Early in this project, Mrs. Miriam Zakon reviewed a sample piece I had submitted and offered important comments, and her involvement toward the end of the project was crucial. I am very grateful. May Hashem comfort her upon the loss of her distinguished husband, Rabbi Nachman Zakon *z"l*.

Thank you to Mrs. Aviva Kohn for the beautiful cover.

My thanks to Rabbi Yitzchok Hisiger for providing me with a number of photographs, and to the well-known photographer of *gedolim*, Moshe D. Yarmish, for allowing the use of his photos. Thank you to Rabbi Tzvi Liberman of Camp Agudah for his help with the photographs.

My appreciation to Mrs. Estie Dicker for her outstanding pagination, and to Mrs. Esther Feierstein for her meticulous proofreading. My thanks as well to the entire staff at ArtScroll/ Mesorah.

May this effort at imparting lessons of *kibbud av va'eim* be a *zechus* for my father and mother *a"h,* as well as for my in-laws *a"h.* It is only a few months since the passing of my dear mother-in-law, Mrs. Marilyn Shapiro *a"h,* who was a beloved mother, grandmother, and great-grandmother to her many descendants. תנצב"ה.

Whatever I accomplish is thanks to my wife, Tova תחי'. May Hashem continue to show us His kindness לאריכת ימים טובים.

I thank the *Ribbono shel Olam* for granting me the *siyata diShmaya* to undertake and complete this project. Rav Aharon Leib Shteinman *zt"l* said that our fulfillment of the mitzvah of *kibbud av va'eim* can give us the power to triumph over our adversaries in *Galus Edom,* whose end we anxiously anticipate. May it come soon, in our time.

Shimon Finkelman

Tammuz 5782/July 2022

Note to the reader: Any name with an asterisk (*) is a fictitious name.

Part 1
Stories

Chapter One
Kibbud Opportunities

The Sky's the Limit

The day was ending in Yerushalayim and the beautiful blue sky was giving way to darkness. Rabbi Moshe Turk, a well-known *talmid chacham* in Yerushalayim, was walking home when something caught his attention. "Why is Chaim* holding a cup of water and looking up at the sky?" Rabbi Turk wondered. Curious, he approached the boy, a neighbor of his, and asked him to explain. Rabbi Turk was amazed at his reply.

"Tonight," Chaim said with excitement, "I'm becoming a bar mitzvah. My rebbi taught us that the reward for someone who does a mitzvah when he's commanded to do it is greater than one who does it when he's not commanded.

"Until now, whenever I did the mitzvah of *kibbud av va'eim,* I did so as a child who wasn't yet commanded to do mitzvos. But tonight when three medium stars come out and night begins, I'll be a bar mitzvah and will be commanded by Hashem to do all mitzvos. So I'm waiting for that moment when night begins and then I'll immediately bring my father this cup of water!"

Rabbi Turk came home and told his children what he had

"All gedolim who became great excelled in their kibbud av va'eim."

heard. Then he added, "*Kinderlach,* I am positive that a boy like Chaim who understands the importance of the holy mitzvah of *kibbud av va'eim* will grow to become a great *talmid chacham* and will teach Torah to many talmidim."

It is now many years since that evening. Rabbi Turk's prediction has been fulfilled, and Reb Chaim* has also written *sefarim* on most *masechtos* in *Shas.*

> *A person can always improve. Even in old age a person can do teshuvah. But it is best for a person to "get things right" when he is young, especially with the mitzvah of kibbud av va'eim. Boys and girls who get used to helping their parents whenever possible and speaking respectfully to them at all times will have prepared themselves for life in how to fulfill one of the Torah's greatest mitzvos.*
>
> *Rabbi Aharon Leib Shteinman told his grandson Rabbi Gedaliah Honigsberg: "If you do a study, you'll discover that all gedolim who became great excelled in their kibbud av va'eim."*

Bread of Blessing

"You think she doesn't like salad?"

"Of course she likes salad — everyone does!"

"I'm going to ask her about it. I'm sure she won't mind if I ask."

For many years, Rebbetzin Aliza Zilberstein, a daughter of Rabbi Yosef Shalom Elyashiv, was a beloved *morah* in a Bais Yaakov school in Bnei Brak. During the lunch break, every *morah* would come to the teachers' room to eat her lunch. Rebbetzin Zilberstein was the only *morah* who had bread with her lunch — every single day. Most of the teachers had salad and fruit, while a few brought some crackers as well, but no one else brought bread.

When the rebbetzin was asked why she always ate bread, she answered:

> *My parents, Rav and Rebbetzin Elyashiv, live in Yerushalayim, and I don't visit them as often as I'd like. So every day, I do something for them here in Bnei Brak by eating bread. If I eat bread, then of course I have to say Bircas HaMazon at the end of my meal. And this gives me the opportunity to say "HaRachaman Hu yevareich es avi mori v'es imi morasi...*

Rebbetzin Zilberstein found a very special way to honor her parents, Rabbi and Rebbetzin Elyashiv, each and every day.

(May the Compassionate One bless my father, my guide, and my mother, my guide...)."

If I can't honor my parents in person, at least I can say a berachah for them from far away.

Always on His Mind (I)

As *menahel* of Yeshivah Torah Vodaath, Rabbi Dovid Bender was a very busy man. But he was never too busy to give pleasure to his father. After his mother passed away and his father lived alone, Rav Dovid would often ask himself, "What can I do today to bring a smile to my father's face?"

Now, you might think that Rav Dovid lived around the corner from his father. In fact, he lived *across the ocean.* His father lived in Eretz Yisrael in the city of Bnei Brak, and Rav Dovid lived in Brooklyn. He was his father's only child, and his father was always on his mind.

If they would be alive today when overseas phone calls are not expensive, Rav Dovid would surely call his father at least once a day. But in those days (the 1950s and '60s) such phone

Rav Dovid used every opportunity to bring pleasure to his father.

calls were very expensive and had to be arranged in advance by calling the phone company.

So Rav Dovid wrote letters — a few times a week. Every six weeks, he would gather his children and tell them, "Today the photographer is coming so that we can take pictures to send to Zeidy."

Every time a child brought home a test with a good mark, a good report card, or a good note from the *rebbi* or *morah*, Rav Dovid would say, "Wonderful! We're going to mail it to Zeidy."

There was great excitement in the Bender home when Zeidy was scheduled to arrive from Eretz Yisrael for a visit. The house was scrubbed clean until it was gleaming from every corner. On the day before Zeidy's arrival, Rav Dovid told his children, "Tomorrow we'll wear Shabbos clothing in honor of Zeidy's arrival. And we'll head for the airport a couple of hours before the plane is scheduled to land to make sure we get there on time."

In those days, there was no security at airports; visitors could take an elevator to an outdoor observation deck and watch the plane land. The Bender family was there well before the plane landed. When it did, Rav Dovid stood on the observation deck craning his neck so that he could catch a glimpse of his father as soon as he emerged from the plane.

And suddenly — there he was! Rav Dovid could not restrain himself. "Papa! Papa!" he shouted. Heads turned to look at the grown man who was shouting with the excitement of a young child.

Rav Dovid ignored the stares. He was focused on one thing — bringing pleasure to his father whom he loved so much.

Rabbi Avrohom Bender heard the shouts and looked up. When he caught sight of his son surrounded by his children, Rav Avrohom broke into a wide, beautiful smile. His son surely brought him tremendous *nachas* and joy.

Always On His Mind (II)

It was on a flight from Tel Aviv to New York following the Knessiah Gedolah (World Conference of Agudas Yisrael) held in Yerushalayim in 1980. Sitting next to each other in the first-class section were Rabbi Yaakov Kamenetsky, a great Rosh Yeshivah and leader of *Klal Yisrael,* and Mr. Yerucham Mashel, a non-religious Jew who was head of the Histadrut, the Israeli labor organization.

Their conversation was interrupted every half-hour or so by a man who appeared to be in his forties and who kept asking Rav Yaakov, "Is there anything you need? Is there something I can get you?" There was also a young woman who came over every so often to ask Rav Yaakov if there was something he needed.

Finally, Mr. Mashel said, "I assume that these people are your aides who came along on the trip with you."

"Actually," replied Rav Yaakov, "they're not my aides. The man is my youngest child who came along on my trip to Eretz Yisrael so that he could help me. The young woman is my grand daughter, who lives in Eretz Yisrael and is coming to America for a visit."

Mr. Mashel was shocked. "Really? Your son is so close to you? I hardly ever see my children — and my grandchildren? Never!"

Rav Yaakov, who was famous for his wisdom, smiled and replied, "Let me explain the difference. We religious Jews look at the giving of the Torah at Sinai as the most important moment in our nation's history. We look at the generation that received the Torah as the greatest ever. The closer we are to the Giving of the Torah, the greater we are. My children and grandchildren look at me with so much respect because I connect them with earlier generations.

"Unfortunately, you probably believe in evolution — that Man came from apes. So why should your children respect you just because you are older?"

Had Mr. Mashel seen just how much Rav Yaakov's children honored him and took care of him in his later years, he would have been even more amazed. His son Reb Avrohom, the one who accompanied him on that trip, set an example for all of us to follow.

Twenty years before he passed away, Rav Yaakov moved to Monsey, while Reb Avrohom lived in Flatbush, which was an hour-and-a-half drive away. Every Wednesday, Reb Avrohom took off an entire day from work so that he could learn with his father and spend time with him. (His mother had passed away many years earlier.) He would tell his children, "I have many more years left when I can work, but I don't know how many years I have left for *kibbud av*."

Every Motza'ei Shabbos, as soon as *Havdalah* ended, the first thing Reb Avrohom did was to call his father. When his father came to visit and the children got home from school, Reb Avrohom would tell them, "First greet Zeidy, then you can greet me."

A few years before Rav Yaakov passed away, he suffered a stroke. From then until the rest of his life, he needed special care. At some point it was decided that Rav Yaakov should move into Reb Avrohom's house in Flatbush. Until Rav Yaakov passed away, Reb Avrohom's life revolved around his father's.

Reb Avrohom traveled to Monsey every week to spend a day with his father.

At some point, when Rav Yaakov needed even more care, Reb Avrohom did not go to the office to run his business. He wanted to be home so that he would always be available for his father. In those days before internet, he conducted his business as best as he could from his house phone. He probably lost some clients because of this, but this did not bother him in the least. No amount of money could be more important than caring for his father.

Around six weeks before Rav Yaakov passed away, it was decided that he should be moved to the home of his daughter and son-in-law, Rabbi and Mrs. Hirsch Diskind, in Baltimore. During that period, Reb Avrohom traveled to Baltimore three times a week to visit his beloved father.

Reb Avrohom certainly valued the mitzvah of *kibbud av va'eim.*

A Home for the Glass

Mrs. Edith Richman* was an outstanding artist who used her talents to bring honor to Hashem's Name. When her shul was planning a new building, she volunteered to design magnificent stained-glass windows that added much beauty to the shul.

Years passed, the neighborhood changed, and the shul could longer find enough Jews for a *minyan*. The property was sold and the building was scheduled to be bulldozed. Mrs. Richman's family was upset. "Our mother put her heart and soul into those windows. We're not going to allow them to become a pile of glass chips. We'll pay to have them removed from the building before the bulldozing and then put them into storage. Maybe someday we'll find some use for them." The windows were removed, carefully wrapped in white sheets, and placed into storage.

When Mrs. Richman passed away, her windows were still in storage. But her family did not forget about them. They were always hoping that they could donate the windows to a shul or yeshivah that was constructing a new building.

Her stained-glass windows were used in the Bostoner Rebbe's shul in Yerushalayim.

And then it happened.

Mrs. Richman's granddaughter Susan became close to the Bostoner Rebbe, Rabbi Levi Yitzchak Horowitz, and Rebbetzin Raichel Horowitz. With her family's approval, she presented the windows to the Rebbe. "I hope that someday the Rebbe will be able to make use of these windows in his shul," she said.

That finally happened in the mid-1980s when the Rebbe opened a shul in Yerushalayim in addition to his shul in Boston. For the next twenty-five years, the Rebbe spent half a year in Boston and half a year in Yerushalayim. The Rebbe was very happy to install Mrs. Richman's stained-glass windows in his new shul in Eretz Yisrael.

Susan called her father with the exciting news. "Daddy, it's finally happening. Grandma's windows are going to be in a shul — and not just any shul. They will be used in the Bostoner Rebbe's new shul in the holy city of Yerushalayim!"

"Susan, that is such great news!" said her father as he cried tears of joy.

Susan brought great joy to her father in this world and to her grandmother in the Next World.

The Surprise Breakfast

"It's okay," said Ezzy.* "I don't want to have it if Ima can't be there."

A few weeks before his bar mitzvah, Ezzy's mother had undergone major emergency surgery. The surgery was successful, but it was certain that she would not be able to attend the gala *seudas mitzvah* in a catering hall that was scheduled for the night when Ezzy turned thirteen. Ezzy's parents felt that the *seudah* should be held as scheduled despite his mother's situation.

Ezzy, mature beyond his years, said to his father, "I really appreciate that you and Ima want me to have a bar mitzvah just like my friends. But without Ima there, it won't be the same. I'd rather have just a small, private *seudah* in our house." And that is what they did.

Six months later, as the school year was drawing to a close, Ezzy's classmates at Yeshivah Darchei Torah approached their Rosh Yeshivah, Rabbi Yaakov Bender.

Rav Pam was very happy to participate in Ezzy's bar mitzvah.

"Rebbi, Ezzy never had a bar mitzvah *seudah* like all of us had. Could we make him a surprise bar mitzvah breakfast the last week of the school year?"

Rabbi Bender loved the idea. He arranged for the yeshivah's kitchen to prepare a beautiful breakfast, hired a musician, and had someone on hand to take pictures.

And then something amazing happened.

On the morning of the *seudah,* which was held in the yeshivah's gym (where there was plenty of room for dancing), a *bris milah* was also being celebrated on the campus of Yeshivah Darchei Torah. The *sandak* was none other than the beloved Rosh Yeshivah of Mesivta Torah Vodaath, Rabbi Avraham Yaakov Pam. After the *bris,* Rabbi Bender told Rav Pam about the special bar mitzvah breakfast that was already in progress. Rav Pam was very moved and said that he wanted to participate.

Ezzy, as well as his father and mother, were speechless when the doors of the gym opened and in walked Rav Pam, accompanied by Rabbi Bender. Rav Pam wished Ezzy and his parents *mazel tov* and wished Ezzy's mother a *refuah sheleimah.*

Ezzy had missed out on a large bar mitzvah celebration because of his consideration for his mother. Hashem rewarded him with a beautiful celebration in which the leader of the generation participated and gave him and his mother a heartfelt *berachah.*

Surprise at the Airport

"Good morning. We are scheduled to land at 6:05 a.m. It is cool and sunny in Tel Aviv. We will soon begin our descent. The seat belt sign has been turned on. Please remain in your seats until the plane has come to a full stop and the seat belt sign has been turned off. We thank you for flying El Al."

Rabbi Morgan* was excited. It wasn't often that he visited Eretz Yisrael. And this time, he had children to visit. His son Yonasan had recently begun learning at Yeshivas Mir Yerushalayim, while his daughter Rina and son-in-law Chaim had been living in Yerushalayim since their marriage a year earlier.

"But first things first," Rabbi Morgan thought as he checked his pocket calendar. He had not *davened* Shacharis on the plane because he preferred to *daven* in a shul. The latest time to *daven Shemoneh Esrei* that day was 9:20. If he made it through passport control quickly and his luggage came off the carousel fairly soon, he could be in a taxi by 7:10. If traffic to Yerushalayim was not heavy, he could arrive at his daughter's apartment by 8:15 and have plenty of time to catch a *minyan*.

But things did not work out as planned. At passport control, a family in front of Rabbi Morgan with six children had a problem with two of their passports. At the carousel, his second suitcase was one of the last to appear. By the time he got the suitcase, it was already 8:00. And someone mentioned that there was heavy traffic on the Tel Aviv–Jerusalem highway.

"What should I do?" he wondered. "Probably the safest plan is to *daven* Shacharis in Bnei Brak, which is only a few minutes from Tel Aviv. But I don't know my way around the city. I might have a hard time finding a shul that still has a *minyan* at this hour."

As he wheeled his luggage cart toward the airport exit, he suddenly stopped.

Three people were smiling and waving at him — Rina, Chaim, and Yonasan!

As Rabbi Morgan hugged his children, he could not help but wonder, "What are you doing here? Chaim, when you told me that you were planning to pick me up at the airport, I said not to come. I'm grateful that you're in kollel and that Yonasan is learning in yeshivah, and I didn't want you to lose time from your *limud haTorah*."

Chaim smiled. "I know, Tatty. As soon as I hung up the phone, I called my Rav and asked him if I should obey your instructions and not come to the airport. He said that since this is one of your rare visits to Eretz Yisrael, the right thing is that all three of us should be at the airport to welcome you. So we rented a car, *davened Vasikin,* and here we are!"

Rabbi Morgan was touched. "Speaking of *davening,*" he said, "it's getting late and I need to *daven* Shacharis. Any suggestions?"

"Sure," Yonasan said, "we thought you might need a *minyan,* so we did some research. The Itzkowitz shul in Bnei Brak has its last Shacharis *minyan* starting in about half an hour. We already put the address into our GPS. We should be there in fifteen minutes!"

Rabbi Morgan was soon sitting in the rented car holding his *tallis* bag, grateful for Hashem's many kindnesses, especially that He had granted him and his wife such wonderful children.

A Visit to the Kosel

"A*nd now this word just in: The Israeli Army has captured the Old City of Jerusalem."*

Anyone who was alive in June of 1967 will remember where they were on that unforgettable day when the Jewish people were *zocheh* to reclaim the Old City, including the Kosel HaMaaravi, the Western Wall of the Har HaBayis from which, our *Chazal* teach, the *Shechinah* has never departed.

I remember where I was. It was recess in yeshivah and everyone was talking about the war and how, *baruch Hashem,* the Israeli Army was having great success against our enemies. And then we heard the news about the Old City. And the Kosel. It was like a dream; it was hard to believe it was really happening.

As soon as the war ended and the Israeli government allowed everyone to visit the Kosel, Jews from all over the world streamed to Eretz Yisrael to *daven* at that very holy place. People trembled, many cried, and everyone experienced emotions that are hard to describe.

One man, Rabbi Mordechai Shapiro, who became a famous Rav in America, wrote a letter to his parents after his first time at the Kosel:

Dearest Daddy and Mommy,

The first night I was here, I simply couldn't control myself and at 1:30 a.m. I took a private taxi from Bnei Brak straight to the Kosel. I was there from 2:30 till 4:30 a.m. I davened for you both. May Hakadosh Baruch Hu in His mercy hear all my tefillos!

Daddy and Mommy: It was worth having given birth to me with all the accompanying chevlei leidah (birth pangs) if even only for those minutes at the Kosel. I am forever indebted to you for having brought me into this world so that thirty-nine years later I soared way up out of this world!

With fierce love, deep affection, and heartfelt emotions,

Mordechai

Rabbi Shapiro had taken his first visit to the Kosel and turned it into a most beautiful moment of *kibbud av va'eim* and *hakaras hatov* to his dear parents.

Last Chance (I)

"Sidney, what a surprise! We just saw you this morning at the *bris*!"

"I know, Dad, but I didn't want to wish you 'Happy Birthday' there. I wanted to come special, just for the purpose of wishing you a Happy Birthday. Many more happy and healthy ones, together with Mom."

That morning, the family had gathered for the *bris* of a grandson of Dr. and Mrs. Sidney Glenner. Dr. Glenner's father celebrated his ninety-third birthday that day. The *bris* of his great-grandson was probably the greatest "birthday present" he could hope for.

When Dr. Glenner surprised his parents with his special afternoon visit to their home, his mother said, "Well, now that you're here, it would be a shame for you to leave so quickly. Have a seat, Sidney, while I prepare lunch for the three of us."

And so Dr. Glenner's surprise visit turned into a birthday party of sorts. Both he and his parents were very happy to be enjoying one another's company.

Because his father always went to sleep at a very late hour, Dr. Glenner had an idea that he thought would bring his father some pleasure.

He called his father close to midnight. "Dad," he said with a chuckle, "I just wanted to be the last one to wish you 'Happy Birthday.'"

His father was quiet for a moment. Then he said, "Sidney, you have always been a good son. I love you."

Those words brought Dr. Glenner to tears. "Dad," he said with emotion, "I love you too."

That night, in the middle of the night, Dr. Glenner's phone rang. It was his mother.

"Sidney!" she cried. "Come quick. Dad is having trouble breathing."

Dr. Glenner got to his parents' house as fast as he could. But by the time he got there, his father had passed away.

While Dr. Glenner mourned his father's passing, he was very grateful that he had made that afternoon visit, as well as that late-night phone call.

Last Chance (II)[1]

It was not a hard decision; I knew what I had to do.

For years and years, I celebrated the Purim *seudah* at the Boro Park home of my very special parents, Rav and Rebbetzin

---

1. The person telling this story is a son of Rabbi Label Katz, a distinguished Rav and author of *sefarim*, who passed away in the spring of 5780 (2020).

Rav and Rebbetzin Katz traveled from the Catskills to Boro Park every week to be with his parents for Shabbos.

Label Katz. My father *zt"l* was a Rav and the head of a yeshivah he had founded. He was also the author of some very popular *sefarim*.

He loved the Torah and he loved doing mitzvos.

He had learned at Mesivta Torah Vodaath. A young talmid there once described his first Simchas Torah at the yeshivah:

> *I had never been in a yeshivah for Simchas Torah until my first year at Torah Vodaath as a ninth-grader. It was an amazing experience. What I remember most is watching a bachur named Label Katz — I was told he was the best bachur in the yeshivah at that time. He did not stop dancing with the Torah and in front of the Torah from the beginning of the first hakafah until the end of the last hakafah. He was smiling and his face was shining the whole time. His suit was soaked with sweat as he danced up a storm. It was a sight that will remain with me forever.*

My father's Purim *seudah* was very lively, full of singing, *divrei Torah,* and dancing. For many years after I was married, we traveled to Brooklyn to be at the *seudah;* I didn't want to miss it. But when I had not only a family of my own but also *talmidim,* I felt that the time had come to host my own Purim *seudah.*

I called my parents to ask for their permission. They not only gave permission, they said that I was doing the right thing. I felt much better after hearing that. Even so, my wife and I decided that our family should join my parents for the Shabbos before Purim, *Shabbos Parashas Zachor.*

The Friday night *seudah* was beautiful. When it ended, my wife called me aside. She wanted me to know that when she had passed by the kitchen in the middle of the meal, she heard my mother telling my sister that Purim would not be the same without me.

I was stunned. I knew that my parents enjoyed having me at their Purim *seudah,* but I had not realized how much it meant to them.

Without wasting a moment, I decided that if my coming for the *seudah* meant so much to them, I would cancel my plans and come to Boro Park as I did every year. My sister tried to talk me out of it. "It's true that Mommy said that, but she understands why it's important for you to make your own *seudah* at home."

My mother also tried to convince me that I should not change my plans.

But I knew what I had to do. I had to take a lesson from my wonderful father and mother, who excelled in the mitzvah of *kibbud av va'eim.*

"Tatty, where are you going?"

"I'm going to see if Bubby or Zeidy need something."

"But you just went over to them a couple of hours ago!"

"I know, but maybe they need something now."

When I was growing up, my mother's parents lived in our

house and my father's parents lived across the street. My father never wasted a moment; if he wasn't answering halachah questions or giving *shiurim*, he was learning. But he still found the time to cross the street a few times a day to check on his elderly parents and see if they needed anything.

For many years, my parents spent their summers at Camp Ohr Shraga, where my father would deliver halachah *shiurim* to hundreds of *bachurim*. He loved spending Shabbos in the pure, uplifting *ruach* of the camp. But when his parents aged and needed even more care, he and my mother would travel from the Catskills to Boro Park *every week* to be with his parents for Shabbos. They did this for ten years.

When I was eleven years old, my grandfather was very sick. My brother's *aufruf* was going to take place in Lakewood and my father did not want to go because he was afraid that something might happen over Shabbos. But the doctor told him, "Rabbi Katz, you have nothing to worry about. Your father's vital signs are good. Nothing bad will happen to him over the weekend." With a heavy heart, my father packed the car and we drove to Lakewood.

That Friday night, I was sitting next to my father in shul. In the middle of *Kabbalas Shabbos,* he turned to me with tears streaming down his face. "*Daven* for Zeidy *now,*" he urged. "He needs your *tefillos*."

As soon as Shabbos ended, we received the news that Zeidy had passed away. He had been taken to the hospital on Friday shortly after sunset, at the time when my father had urged me to *daven* for Zeidy. My father's *neshamah* had sensed that something was happening to his father at that time.

So now you understand why *kibbud av va'eim* is so important to me — I grew up watching how important this mitzvah was to my father and mother. So when I heard that my mother would miss having me at the Purim *seudah,* there was no question in my mind about what to do.

After Shabbos, I notified my *talmidim* and others that we had changed our plans and would not be home for Purim. They fully understood, and everyone made other arrangements.

The Purim *seudah* at my parents' house was as beautiful and lively as ever. There was a lot of singing and dancing, especially at the end when I danced with my father as we sang one of his favorite *niggunim, Achakeh Lo,* about our longing for Mashiach.

That was the last time I saw my father.

A few days after Purim, people began getting sick with Covid. My father was hospitalized and none of us were allowed to visit him. He passed away shortly thereafter.

Tatty, who knows how many extra years were granted to you because of your amazing *kibbud av va'eim?*

Tatty, how grateful I am that I spent that Purim *seudah* with you and Mommy!

Now, I await Mashiach and *techiyas hameisim* when we will see each other once again.

A Perfect Shirt

"Are you sure, Tatty?"

"Yes, I'm sure, Dovid. Please do a good job."

The year was 1939. The German army had invaded Poland and begun what they called "The Final Solution," their evil plan to get rid of every last Jew in the world. In every Polish town that they invaded, they ordered all Jews — men, women, and children — to come to the center of town. From there, the Germans claimed, the Jews would be "relocated to labor camps."

In most cases, they were deported to concentration camps, where the vast majority were killed. Only a small percentage survived the horrors of those camps.

When the town in which Dovid and his father lived was invaded and orders were given, the Jews were told, "You have two hours to assemble in the town square. Each person may take one small suitcase in which you may put only essentials. Nothing else will be allowed on the train."

"Essentials" meant items such as food, a sweater or toothbrush — things that are very needed for day-to-day living. Some people tried to sew jewelry and other valuables into the lining of their coats.

The people had no idea that the moment they stepped off the train, everything they had brought with them would be taken away. They would be left with nothing.

Dovid understood why his father wanted to pack an extra shirt. But to iron it? What for? At this point in time, did anyone really care if his shirt had a few creases? They were worried about survival, not about neatly pressed shirts.

But that is what Dovid's father wanted, so Dovid took the iron and got to work. It was not often that he ironed, but when he finished, he thought he had done a good job and that his father would be pleased.

Dovid was in for a surprise.

"Dovid, my very dear son, I can see that you tried your best, but if you look here, you'll see that you missed a couple of creases. Please iron it again."

Dovid was stunned. "Tatty, I'm really sorry, but I don't understand. Why is it so important that this shirt should be perfectly pressed? We don't know what the future holds. All we want is to remain alive. Everyone is busy trying to figure out what to take along for survival. Why are you so concerned about this shirt?"

Dovid's father was quiet for a few moments before answering. When he began to speak, there were tears in his eyes.

"Dovid, I know exactly what's happening. I don't need a perfectly pressed shirt. I have a feeling that the 'essentials' we're taking along won't be ours for very long.

"Nothing is certain — except for one thing. The *zechus* of every mitzvah we do is ours forever; no one can take it away from us. And *kibbud av va'eim* is a very great mitzvah. I don't know if you and I will be together once we get off that train, so I'm trying to give you the *zechus* of *kibbud av va'eim* now by asking you to do things for me. It's not the shirt that I need; I need you to have the mitzvah of doing something for me."

Dovid was astounded. He had always looked up to his father, but he had never realized how special his father was. At a time of such fear and uncertainty, his father was thinking about ways to grant him *zechuyos.*

When the war was over, Dovid was the only survivor of his town. Only Hashem knows why he survived, but Dovid felt that it might have to do with his father's perfectly pressed shirt.

Chapter Two
The Right Outlook

"Grab It!"

Reb Yaakov was not sure what to do.

Originally from England, Reb Yaakov had been living in Yerushalayim for many years, where he was a very close *talmid* of Rabbi Dovid Soloveitchik, the great Rosh Yeshivah of Brisk. Rav Dovid was one of the greatest tzaddikim of the generation. Even strangers would ask him for *berachos.* Wherever he went, people would come over to shake his hand and speak to him. He was a very kind, caring person and he took people's suffering very much to heart.

Rav Dovid lived to age 98. As he got older, it became necessary for him to have a *"gabbai,"* someone who would drive him where he needed to go and be at his side to help him with whatever he needed. His *talmid* Reb Yaakov became his *gabbai.* Rav Dovid loved Reb Yaakov and trusted him. He knew that he could rely on him to do whatever needed to be done, and that if something needed to be kept a secret, he would keep a secret.

And then the phone call came from England.

"Yaakov, as you know, at their age, Tatty and Mommy can no longer take care of themselves. They need someone to be with

"Perhaps this is why Hashem has granted me a very long life."

them all the time to help them with whatever they need. Do you think that you could come to England for Pesach to take care of them?"

Reb Yaakov was eager and ready to come to help his parents — but one thought troubled him.

> *Who will take care of Rav Dovid while I'm away? He relies on me for so many things. And Yom Tov is such a busy time. So many people come to visit him and ask for berachos. How can I leave him at such a time?*
>
> *But my parents need me. How can I not help them?*

Reb Yaakov decided to ask Rav Dovid what to do. He knew that when Rav Dovid would hear the question, he would not think to himself, "But how can I tell Reb Yaakov to go — I need him!" A tzaddik does not think about himself when he answers such a question. He tells the person what Hashem wants him to do in that situation.

This is what Rav Dovid told him.

> *As you know, during World War II, my mother was killed, along with some of my siblings. From the day my mother died, I took upon myself to take care of my father. Until I got married, I slept in the same room as him. I never went to sleep before he went to sleep, and I always made sure to*

be up very early so that I would be up when my father got up. There were many nights when my father would learn until two or three o'clock in the morning. I was very tired, but I would not go to sleep as long as my father was still up.

Of course, after I got married, I lived with my wife in another apartment. I could no longer be with my father all the time as before. But I still made sure to visit him two or three times a day.

Perhaps this is why Hashem has granted me a very long life.

And now you have the opportunity to go to England for Yom Tov and take care of your parents — and you're asking me whether or not you should go?

You have such an opportunity for kibbud av va'eim and you want to know what to do? Grab it!

Cheer Up!

The elderly man sitting with Rabbi Aharon Leib Shteinman looked very sad.

He did not want to waste the Rosh Yeshivah's time, so he got straight to the point.

"Rosh Yeshivah," he said with tears in his eyes, "all my life I have given to others, especially my children. Together with my wife, I took care of my children from the day they were born. I placed them in the best yeshivos, I helped them with their learning. I bought them whatever they needed and took them wherever they needed to go. They appreciated this and have given me much *nachas.*

"But now in my old age, I cannot do anything for them anymore. Now, the opposite is true. They do everything for me. They come to my apartment to cook for me, they shop for me,

"But now, in your old age, you are really helping your children!"

they take me to my doctors' appointments. They do everything for me — and I do nothing for them. Oh, Rosh Yeshivah, it is so painful! I used to *give to* my children. Now I *take from* my children."

Reb Aharon Leib looked at this wonderful man with love and compassion. "You are making a mistake," he said softly. "You said that when your children were growing up, you bought them whatever they needed. But was the money really your money? Everything belongs to Hashem, so you were using Hashem's money to help your children.

"But now, in your old age, you are *really* helping your children! How? By giving them so many chances to fulfill the mitzvah of *kibbud av.* Do you know what your son or daughter is earning every time they help you? Do you have any idea what kind of reward Hashem will give them for all that they do for you? There is no way that they can ever pay you back for the mitzvos you are allowing them to earn.

"So cheer up! You are still a giver — a *real* giver!"

The Letter That Wasn't Printed

Rabbi Chaim Kanievsky wrote a small *sefer* on the laws of *mezuzah.* It is common when publishing a *sefer* to ask well-known *talmidei chachamim* to write *haskamos,* letters of endorsement, in which they write that the *sefer* is a good one and is worthy of being studied.

Rav Chaim's plan was to publish two *haskamos,* one from his father, the Steipler Gaon, and one from his father-in-law, Rabbi Yosef Shalom Elyashiv. Rav Elyashiv wrote a beautiful *haskamah.* However, Rav Chaim's father did not write one. He explained that he had a firm rule that he never wrote a *haskamah* on a *sefer* of halachah. Though Rav Chaim was his son, he felt that if he made an exception and wrote a *haskamah* for his *sefer,* people would expect him to write *haskamos* for other *sefarim* as well. He could not break his rule.

Of course, Rav Chaim understood. But he felt that it would

Out of respect for his father, he would not publish the letter.

not be respectful to his father for his *sefer* to be published with a *haskamah* from his father-in-law but not from his father. People would not know the truth, that the Steipler simply could not write a *haskamah*. Some might mistakenly think that Rav Chaim had asked his father-in-law for a letter of *haskamah* but had not asked his father! So out of respect for his father, he did not print Rav Elyashiv's letter.

A Five-Cent Lesson

Rabbi Simcha Dovid Paritzky was a quiet man who was also an outstanding *talmid chacham,* though few people knew it. When he moved to Baltimore, the Rosh Yeshivah of Yeshivas Ner Yisroel, Rabbi Yitzchok Ruderman, got to know him and had tremendous respect for him. In his later years when he would go to Florida for the winter, Rabbi Paritzky was a *chavrusa* of the famous Torah leader Rabbi Yaakov Kamenetsky.

At home, he never raised his voice — almost never. His son, Dr. Michael Paritzky, recalls only one time when he heard his father raise his voice.

"I was around eight years old and I was coloring, sitting on the floor of my father's office, which was in our house. I heard my father tell my mother that someone who owed him money had mistakenly sent him an extra five cents. And he asked her to please mail the five cents to the person.

"My mother didn't understand. 'But it's only five cents,' she said. 'And the stamp on the envelope will cost us three cents. (This was a long time ago; today stamps are much more expensive.) I'm sure he won't mind...'

"That was when my father raised his voice. 'Flora,' he said to my mother, 'please send the man his five cents. I don't care if it's five hundred dollars, fifty dollars, five dollars, fifty cents, or five cents. If it doesn't belong to us, I don't want it.'

"My mother sent the money as my father had requested. That

was the only time I ever heard my father raise his voice, and I never forgot what he said."

Many years later, Dr. Michael Paritzky was a very successful foot and ankle surgeon. He was so successful that one day he decided that he had to expand his office by adding more examination rooms. The renovations would cost $30,000. Dr. Paritzky was able to borrow this amount from a local bank with whom he had a very good relationship. He was to pay back a certain amount every month so that after a few years, the entire sum would be repaid.

One day, Dr. Paritzky was in his office when he received a special envelope from the bank. Inside was a letter that stated that his $30,000 loan had been paid in full. "Today is your lucky day, Doctor," his secretary said.

But Dr. Paritzky did not think so. He found the letter very troubling. "This letter is a mistake," he said. "The loan is not paid up in full. I paid back only $10,000, and I still owe $20,000. The bank made a mistake — a big mistake."

Dr. Paritzky knew that even if the bank discovered that this letter had been sent by mistake, they probably would not be able to demand that he pay back the rest of the loan. He could save himself $20,000, which is quite a large sum.

But Dr. Paritzky did not think for a moment that he should keep the money. That's because, in his mind, he heard his father saying, "I don't care if it's five hundred dollars, fifty dollars, five dollars, fifty cents, or five cents. If it doesn't belong to us, I don't want it."

He told his secretary, "Please arrange for the patients in the waiting room to see one of our other doctors. I must go to the bank right now."

He arrived at the bank and went straight to the office of the president, who knew him well. Dr. Paritzky showed the president the letter he had received from the bank. "It says here that

I paid my loan in full. But I know that I paid only $10,000. I still owe $20,000."

"Are you sure?" asked the president. "Perhaps a friend of yours paid for you without your knowing. Or maybe you simply forgot that you paid."

"No one paid for me," Dr. Paritzky said with confidence. "And I didn't pay it either. Your office made a mistake."

The president then checked the bank records and saw that Dr. Paritzky was right. He still owed $20,000. The bank had made a mistake — a very big mistake.

The president was stunned. "Sir, I have been involved with this bank for many years, and I worked in other banks before that. And I have never met anyone as honest and G-d-fearing as you are."

The president then called together the bank's entire staff and told the story of "the most decent and honorable man I ever met."

Dr. Paritzky's honesty created a great *kiddush Hashem*. To Dr. Paritzky, there was no question that he had to speak up and let the bank know that he owed them the money — because in his mind, he could still hear his father saying, "I don't care if it's five hundred dollars, fifty dollars, five dollars, fifty cents, or five cents. If it doesn't belong to us, I don't want it."

> *Kitzur Shulchan Aruch says that the best way to honor our parents is by learning Torah and doing mitzvos. This is especially true if we do mitzvos because of what we learned from watching our parents. Dr. Paritzky's kiddush Hashem brought great honor to both his father and mother.*

Not for All the Money in the World

The phone rang in the home of Shlomo Simcha Sufrin, a popular singer who lives in Toronto and is known as Shlomo Simcha.

"Shlomo Simcha," the caller said, "my name is Chezky Stein* and I'm a *chassan*. I'm getting married on Lag BaOmer and I would like to hire you to sing at my wedding."

Shlomo Simcha checked his calendar; he had not yet been hired to sing on that night. "That date is open," he told Chezky. "I'll be happy to sing at your wedding." They agreed on a price. Then Shlomo Simcha wrote down where the wedding would take place and what time he was supposed to be there.

The next day, Shlomo Simcha received a phone call from an old customer. "Shlomo Simcha, this is Daniel Miller.* Well, you sang at the weddings of our other sons, and now our youngest son is getting married. The wedding will be on Lag BaOmer."

Mr. Miller was a very wealthy man, and Shlomo Simcha knew that he would pay him a lot more money than Chezky Stein had agreed to pay. But that made no difference. "I'm really sorry, Mr. Miller, but I can't sing at your son's wedding. I already agreed to sing at someone else's wedding on that same night."

Mr. Miller was quiet for a few moments. "I'll tell you what," he finally said, "tell the other fellow that I'll give him $3,000 if he'll allow you to sing at my son's wedding."

Shlomo Simcha called the *chassan*. "I'm sorry," Chezky said, "but I don't agree to this deal. I still want you to sing at my wedding."

But Mr. Miller was not ready to give up. When Shlomo Simcha told him what Chezky had said, Mr. Miller replied, "Tell him that I'll give him $5,000."

Chezky still would not agree to release Shlomo Simcha from their agreement. When Mr. Miller heard this, he said, "Tell him that I'll give him $10,000."

Chezky did not agree.

This time Mr. Miller said, "Look, you sang at the weddings of all my other sons and it added so much to the wedding. We want the same for this son. Tell that fellow that he should name his price. I will give whatever amount of money he wants so that he will allow you to sing at my son's wedding."

When Shlomo Simcha told this to Chezky, he was amazed at his reply. "There is no amount of money that would cause me to release you from our agreement. I want you to sing at my wedding."

"That's fine," Shlomo Simcha said, "I'll sing at your wedding. But if you don't mind my asking, why is it so important to you that I should sing at your wedding? Wouldn't it make more sense to take all this money he's offering you and hire another singer for your wedding?"

This was Chezky's answer:

"My father took ill many years ago and is disabled. All these years, my mother raised us, took care of my father, and also earned money to support the family.

"When I got engaged and we started to plan the wedding, my mother commented, 'It would be so nice if Shlomo Simcha could sing at your wedding.' That's why I hired you. I hired you because that is what my mother wanted. By having you sing at my wedding, I'm expressing my *hakaras hatov* for all that my mother did for all of us all these years.

"And that's why no amount of money can make me change my mind."

Shlomo Simcha was touched by this young man's words. What a beautiful way to show appreciation to a very special mother.

"You're So Special!"

I'm so, so tired. It's Sunday morning again, and I can hardly keep my eyes open. What can I do? I love my father, and he works very hard running his small newspaper stand and candy store. Sunday morning is his big newspaper day, when many people come to buy the special weekly edition of the paper with its many sections. On Motza'ei

Shabbos the papers are delivered to his store, and each section comes in a separate stack. It takes hours to collate the different stacks so that each newspaper is ready to be sold early Sunday morning.

When I turned twelve, my father told me, "Yossi, you're growing up and I'm getting older. It's getting hard for me to put together those newspapers by myself. I need you to help me. I know that you'll be tired the next day, and I feel bad about it. I know it will be hard for you to concentrate in yeshivah on Sunday. But I have no one else to ask."

So for the past two years, I've been doing it. Now, I'm in ninth grade and I love the learning. My rebbi, Rabbi Dovid Trenk, is a great rebbi and makes learning so exciting. But what can I do? Every Sunday, I will feel like a big failure. I will hardly hear what he is saying. Sometimes, I will actually put my head down and fall asleep.

On the first Sunday morning of that school year, Rabbi Trenk called Yossi over to his desk after class. "Yossi," he said with a smile, "it's such a pleasure to have you in my class. I see you really want to learn and I'm sure you're going to do great. But I noticed you were very tired today. Were you up very late last night?"

Rabbi Trenk told Yossi: "You're a special son and a special talmid!"

In tears, Yossi told his rebbi his story. When he finished, Rabbi Trenk hugged him and said, "Yossi, you are so special! What an amazing mitzvah of *kibbud av*! We will work together to figure out a way that you shouldn't be so tired on Sunday mornings. Maybe you should *daven* in a shul near your house and take a nap before coming to yeshivah. But don't feel bad about what you're doing — be proud! You're a special son and a special *talmid*!"

Yossi went home that day feeling good and confident about the future. If he was a special son and special talmid, it was because he had special parents and a special rebbi.

Cookies and Ices

"Did you notice that Tatty doesn't eat cake or cookies anymore?"

"Yes... maybe he's trying to eat only healthy foods."

Rabbi Zvi Karmel was a beloved father, son, and rebbi. No one knew the real reason for his "new diet" until his mother passed away. During the week of *shivah* following her passing, Rabbi Karmel helped himself to a piece of a Danish. When one of his sons asked, "But Tatty, I thought you don't eat cake anymore?" tears welled in Rabbi Karmel's eyes.

"Bubby is now at peace," he told his son, "so I can eat my Danish in peace."

His mother had been ill for quite a while. The day came when she could no longer eat or drink; she had to be nourished through an intravenous tube. One day, she told her son that she missed having her morning cup of coffee that "got her going" and which she enjoyed.

It was then that Rabbi Karmel made a decision. "If my mother cannot enjoy her coffee, then I will not enjoy cake or cookies."

Only after she passed away and was "at peace" did he taste a Danish.

To be nosei b'ol, to feel the pain of another Jew, is a very

"Take a picture of me and show it to him."

special and important middah. This is especially true when the person in pain is our own father or mother.

Or grandfather or grandmother.

The last chapter of ArtScroll's magnificent biography of Rabbi Meir Zlotowitz tells of how his family stayed with him around the clock when he was hospitalized during his final days. His children and grandchildren who were not at the hospital were *davening* for him at home.

One of his young grandsons was sitting on the couch at home saying *Tehillim* for his zeidy. He called his mother, who was visiting at the hospital, and said, "Mommy, I just finished saying all fifteen of the *Shir HaMaalos* in *Tehillim.*"

"That's wonderful, Yoni!"* she said. She complimented him and told him to help himself to ices from the freezer.

"How can I eat ices if Zeidy is sick?" the boy asked.

His mother shared the conversation with her father. Rabbi Zlotowitz had an idea. "Take a picture of me and show it to him. He'll see that I'm okay and he'll enjoy the ices." And that is what his daughter did.

And then Yoni ate his ices.

A Lesson From Yosef HaTzaddik

The year was 1962. Chaim Dovid Ackerman, a *bachur* who lived in the United States, had spent two years learning in Eretz Yisrael *without ever going home*! And now he was finally going home to spend Yom Tov with his family. Today, it is common for a *bachur* learning in Eretz Yisrael to come home every Pesach, and sometimes for Succos as well. But in those days, not many boys went from America to learn in Eretz Yisrael, and those who did go did not come home that often. It was too expensive.

Chaim Dovid was learning at the famous Chevron Yeshivah in Yerushalayim. The yeshivah had *talmidim* from all over the world, including England. When Chaim Dovid made plans to fly home, his friends said to him, "Chaim Dovid, why not spend a few days in London with us on your way home? You've never been to London — we'll give you a grand tour!"

Chaim Dovid was excited by this invitation. He called his parents, who told him that if that was what he wanted to do, it was fine with them. Before long, his plane was touching down at Heathrow Airport in London. Chaim Dovid was really looking forward to this visit.

On Friday, one of Chaim Dovid's friends told him, "You'll never believe who is giving a *shmuess* tonight in one of the local shuls — Rav Sholom Schwadron, the *chazzan* on Rosh Hashanah and Yom Kippur in our yeshivah!"

Rav Sholom was not just a *chazzan,* he was also a *maggid*. A *maggid* is a *talmid chacham* who gives speeches in public that are filled with words of *mussar* and interesting stories, stories that teach people how to be better Jews. Rav Schwadron was a master at his trade. In fact, Rabbi Paysach Krohn's first "Maggid book" was *The Maggid Speaks: Favorite Stories and Parables of Rabbi Sholom Mordechai Schwadron.* Many people's lives were changed forever from hearing a *mussar shmuess* from Rav Schwadron, the "Maggid of Yerushalayim."

Chaim Dovid entered the shul that Friday night tingling with excitement. It was the week of *Parashas Vayigash,* which relates how Yosef HaTzaddik reveals himself to his brothers and then has his long-awaited reunion with his father, Yaakov Avinu. Rav Schwadron was sure to have something interesting to say.

He certainly did. This is what he said:

Yosef HaTzaddik was separated from his father for twenty-two years, until they were finally reunited in Mitzrayim. The Torah says that when Yaakov Avinu finally arrived, "Yosef appeared to him" (Bereishis 46:29). Rashi explains: "Yosef appeared to his father."

Rashi never wastes words. He is always teaching us something that we might not have known. What is he teaching us by saying, "Yosef appeared to his father"? Isn't that what the pasuk says?

To understand the answer to this question, we have to ask ourselves a question. What should Yosef have been thinking as he was heading to the reunion with his father? What would the average son be thinking as he was about to see his beloved father whom he had not seen in twenty-two years? Most people would probably be thinking, "I can't wait to see my father!"

Yosef, however, had a different thought. He was thinking, "I can't wait for ***my father*** *to see* ***me****! My father has missed me so much. He has suffered so much. I can't wait to bring him pleasure when I appear before him."*

This is what Rashi means when he says, "Yosef appeared to his father."

Chaim Dovid could not believe what he had just heard. It was as if Rav Schwadron was telling him, "Why are you spending time in London with friends when your parents have not seen you in two years? Shouldn't you be thinking about the pleasure you'll give them by coming home? Why are you postponing your reunion with your parents, who care about you so much?"

Sunday morning, Chaim Dovid took the first available flight to America "to appear before his parents" and give them *nachas.*

The Chofetz Chaim Comes to Town

The city of Vilna was abuzz with excitement. The leader of the generation, Rabbi Yisroel Meir HaKohen Kagan, better known as the Chofetz Chaim, was coming for a visit. There was going to be a huge *kabbalas panim,* reception, where everyone would get a chance to pass by the Chofetz Chaim and, if he was not too tired, shake his hand.

In the Rameilles Yeshivah, it was announced that the *rebbeim* and all the *talmidim* would participate in the *kabbalas panim.* The boys were counting the days until the moment when they would get to see the *gadol hador.*

The day before the Chofetz Chaim's arrival, Shabsi Goldman,* who lived in another city, received a letter from his father.

> *Dear Shabsi:*
>
> *We hope that you are well and that you are progressing in your learning. My dear Shabsi, I have heard the news that the leader of the generation, the Chofetz Chaim, is coming*

He felt that the Chofetz Chaim would have told him that he did the right thing by obeying his father's instructions.

to Vilna. I have also heard that there will be a grand kabbalas panim where all the Jews of the city will gather to greet the tzaddik.

Shabsi, I am afraid for you to participate in that gathering. There will be thousands of people there, and there will probably be a lot of pushing in a crowded area. You are very thin and not tall, and you might get hurt, chas v'shalom.

Shabsi, I know how badly you want to see the Chofetz Chaim, but I am asking you to obey your father's instructions and remain in the beis midrash of your yeshivah even as the other bachurim go to take part in that gathering.

Thank you for always being the most wonderful son.

With so much love,

Tatty

Shabsi read the letter a few times. He was terribly disappointed. He wanted so much to see the Chofetz Chaim. And everyone else was going! But he would not disobey his father.

On the day of the Chofetz Chaim's arrival, the entire Rameilles Yeshivah attended the *kabbalas panim* — except for Shabsi Goldman, who remained in the beis midrash learning. When the grand reception was over, the *bachurim* returned to the yeshivah, and Shabsi's classmates had a lot to say.

"Oh, Shabsi, what you missed! It was unbelievable! Our whole class stood in front of the Chofetz Chaim — we got to see him from up close. And that's not all — he gave all of us a *berachah* for *arichas yamim* (long life). What a shame you weren't there!"

Shabsi felt bad, but he did not regret listening to his father. He felt that the Chofetz Chaim would have told him that he did the right thing by obeying his father's instructions.

Years passed. Europe became engulfed in World War II, and the majority of the Jews of Vilna were killed. Shabsi survived the war and made his way to Eretz Yisrael. He managed to make contact with some of his former classmates who had survived the war, and kept in touch with them.

All of them lived to a ripe old age, just as the Chofetz Chaim had blessed them. And Shabsi Goldman, who had the Torah's *berachah* for those who honor their parents, outlived them all.

A Special Seder

Like every adult, I have special memories of my parents' Seder table. My parents, Reb Shmuel Avigdor and Mrs. Selma Finkelman, struggled to pay their monthly bills, but our Seder table always looked beautiful. When my mother had the opportunity to choose a gift of silver from her employers, she chose a magnificent *Kos Shel Eliyahu* that she placed in the center of the table. That *kos* is now one of my most precious possessions and has adorned my Seder table for many years.

One Seder at my parents' home stands out in my mind — not because of what took place, but because of what *did not* take place.

Like all children, my brothers and sisters and I would come home from school before Yom Tov excited to share all that we had learned about Pesach and the *Haggadah.* One year, Bubby, my father's mother, came to spend Yom Tov with us. Bubby was old and frail; not long after Pesach it became clear that her mind was not the same, and it eventually was necessary for her to live in a nursing home.

That year, before the Seder began, my father told us children, "Bubby is here and she is not able to stay up very late. But she wants to be at the Seder. So we'll have to make the Seder much shorter than we usually do."

I remember how disappointed I was. Besides not being able to share all my *divrei Torah,* I knew that when we came back to yeshivah after Yom Tov, my classmates would announce how late their Seder ended. The later it ended, the prouder the boy was. And now, I probably would have the shortest Seder of all!

Of course, we did as my father said. Years later, I thought about that Seder and realized how right he had been.

My father excelled in his *kibbud eim.* He worked long, hard hours and usually arrived home at about 6:30. My grandmother lived nearly two miles away and my parents did not own a car. Yet my father made sure to visit his mother often, even when her mind was not clear and she did not even recognize members of her own family.

My father also showed great respect for his mother-in-law, my other grandmother. After my grandfather passed away, "Bobby" would come to us for Shabbos very often. She would bring a treat for her grandchildren and a special treat for my father. It was obvious that she thought very highly of him and appreciated the way he honored her. She also appreciated what a good husband he was to my mother.

And when my mother was out of earshot, my grandmother would tell us, "Your mother is such a good daughter. She takes care of everything I need and is never too busy to help me whenever I need her."

Packing Our Parachutes

Mr. Charles Plumb is a former pilot in the United States Navy. During the war in Vietnam in the 1960s, Mr. Plumb flew an F-4 Phantom jet on seventy-four successful combat missions. On May 19, 1967, during his seventy-fifth mission, just five days before he was to return home, Charles' jet was shot out of the sky by a surface-to-air missile. He parachuted to the ground and was then captured and imprisoned by the North Vietnamese. He spent the next 2,103 days as a prisoner of war.

In 1973, Charles Plumb was released by his captors and

returned to flying jets for the Navy. Eventually, he retired with a rank of captain after thirty-one years of service.

Charles and his wife were once sitting in a restaurant in Kansas City. Two tables over, a man kept looking at him, as if he knew him, but Charles didn't recognize the man.

The fellow walked over to Charles' table and pointed at him.

"You're Captain Plumb, aren't you?" asked the stranger.

"Yes, sir," Charles confirmed.

"You're that guy! You flew jet fighters in Vietnam from the aircraft carrier *Kitty Hawk*. You were shot down."

"That is correct," Charles replied.

"You parachuted into enemy hands and spent six years as a prisoner of war."

"Yes, that's me," said Charles. "How in the world do you know all this?"

The man smiled. "Because I prepared your parachute before you took off on that mission."

Charles was speechless.

Shaking Charles' hand, the man said, "I guess the parachute worked!"

"It sure did," said a grateful Charles Plumb. "If it hadn't, I wouldn't be alive today."

"Did you keep track of all the parachutes you packed?" asked Charles. "Do you know of all the lives you've saved?"

"No," said the man humbly. "I never kept track of all the parachutes I packed. But I happened to have known that I packed yours on the day when you got shot down."

That night, Charles Plumb couldn't sleep. He was filled with guilt. How many times had he passed this sailor on their ship and not even greeted him with a "Good morning"? After all, Charles Plumb was a fighter pilot and this man was just a sailor.

Charles tossed and turned, imagining that man in a sailor's uniform, sitting at a long wooden table on the ship and, with his nimble fingers, carefully folding his parachute, making sure that it was ready for use if need be.

That sailor's work was hardly noticed, but the parachutes he prepared saved the lives of Charles Plumb and many others who had to parachute to safety. He had saved many people who did not know his name and therefore could never give him what he richly deserved — a proper thank you.

Charles Plumb often says, "Everyone has someone in his life who 'packs his parachute,' who gives him the tools he needs to live a healthy, productive life. Does he ever tell that person a proper thank you?"

> *A Torah Jew knows that there is no person to whom he owes more gratitude than his father and mother. They "pack his parachute" in so many ways, from the moment he is born and even after he becomes an adult. A child can always count on his parents in his time of need.*
>
> *There are many opportunities to say thank you to a parent. After a meal, remember to say thank you to your mother. When she hands you your clean laundry, remember to say thank you. When your father learns with you, drives you somewhere, helps you with something, remember to say thank you.*

"Thank You" to the Seamstress

"Yes, it's very beautiful. It is a *kavod* for the *aron kodesh* and a *kavod* for the *Sifrei Torah*."

A *talmid* had accompanied Rabbi Shlomo Freifeld, Rosh Yeshivah of Yeshivah Sh'or Yoshuv in Far Rockaway, to purchase a new *paroches* for the yeshivah's *aron kodesh*. They had found a beautiful antique *paroches* that had been made in India many years ago.

"It's beautiful, but it does need some mending. Let's ask the store owner about having it fixed."

The man assured them that his seamstress was outstanding and would have the *paroches* looking as good as new.

Sometime later, Rav Freifeld and his *talmid* returned to the store to pick up the *paroches*. Rav Freifeld was very pleased. "It's beautiful," he told the store owner. "I am so pleased. Would you allow me to go to the back of the store so that I can thank the seamstress?"

The man was touched that this great Rabbi would want to take the time for this. He led him to the back of the store, where Rav Freifeld warmly thanked the seamstress for her outstanding work.

Many years later, after Rav Freifeld passed away, the seamstress told his son-in-law Rabbi Naftoli Jaeger, "For forty years I worked in the back of the store making things beautiful, but no one ever noticed. But when your father-in-law picked up the *paroches*, he insisted on coming to the back of the store to thank me personally, telling me how magnificent my work was and how beautiful the *paroches* would look when it hung on the yeshivah's *aron kodesh*."

Great people make sure to thank those to whom they owe appreciation.

"Would you allow me to go to the back of the store to thank the seamstress?"

The Secret

"How does Naftali do it?"

"I don't know; it doesn't make any sense."

Naftali was a *talmid* in the beis midrash of the Gateshead Yeshivah in Gateshead, England. He was a serious, well-liked *bachur* who applied himself to his learning as best as he could. Other boys were considered smarter, sharper, with better memories. When the rebbi asked a hard question, Naftali's hand was usually not the one that shot up to answer it.

The strange thing was that year after year, when it was time for the boys to arrange for a *chavrusa* for the coming *zeman* (term), Naftali *always* got the best *chavrusa*! The top *bachurim,* the ones who understood the Gemara the best, wanted to learn with him. And Naftali was thrilled. Because this meant that if there was something he did not understand in the Gemara, his *chavrusa* would probably know it and be able to explain it.

But why did he always end up with the best *chavrusa*? No one could figure it out. Until one day...

It was during the final days of the *zeman*. That day, the *bachurim* had been busy finding *chavrusos* for the coming *zeman.* Toward the end of the day, someone overheard Naftali on the phone.

"Mommy, this is Naftali. Thank you so much for saying Tehillim that I should get good chavrusos. Baruch Hashem, I got very good chavrusos for next zeman."

Naftali and his mother believed in the power of a *tefillah,* especially the heartfelt *tefillah* of a mother for the sake of her son.

Children have no idea how many *tefillos* their parents say for their sake, how many tears they shed. They *daven* for them from the day they are born and never stop.

Rabbi Manis Mandel was a beloved tzaddik and *mechanech.* After his last child was engaged, one of his older daughters said

Rabbi Mandel never stopped davening for his children.

to him, "Tatty, aren't you relieved now that you will have married off all your children?"

Rabbi Mandel replied that of course, he was very grateful to Hashem for bringing him to this wonderful moment in his life. "But," he told his daughter, "do you think that I stopped *davening* for you when you got married? After your wedding, I also *davened* for your husband, and then when your children were born, I started to *daven* for them. And I will continue to *daven* for all of you."

When Rabbi Chaim Kanievsky was sixty years old, his father, the Steipler Gaon, told someone, "Not a day goes by that I don't shed tears for my Chaim."

The "Thank You" Mitzvah

In fact, the mitzvah of *kibbud av va'eim* is a mitzvah of saying "Thank you."

Sefer HaChinuch writes that honoring parents is a way of expressing gratitude for all that a parent does for his or her child. Every time that we honor our parents by bringing them their food, helping them with their chores, or assisting them in other ways, we are expressing our appreciation to them. And, when we appreciate our parents, we will also come to appreciate all that Hashem does for us every day of our lives.

No matter how much we honor our parents, there is no way that we can ever repay them for all that they have done for us.

Very often, children express their gratitude by celebrating their parents' anniversary with a party.

The Big "Celebration"

"It's not just any anniversary," Esther* told her sister Miriam,* "it's Daddy and Mommy's *fiftieth* anniversary! It calls for something special."

Esther and Miriam contacted their brothers and sisters, and after a decision was made, Yaakov Gerstein,* the oldest of the children, was elected to make the phone call.

"Daddy, hi, it's Yaakov. I have some exciting news. Could Mommy pick up the other phone?"

His mother was soon on the phone, and Yaakov began. "Daddy and Mommy, you know that there is no way in the world that we children can ever repay you for all that you've done for us. But since it will soon be your fiftieth wedding anniversary, we wanted to do something really special as a small token of our appreciation. We decided that since it's something really big and expensive, we should let you know in advance just in case there is some reason you wouldn't want it.

"We're all chipping in and renting a hall for a grand anniversary party! We're going to invite not only your children and grandchildren, but also your brothers and sisters and their children! And we're going to plan a whole program with speeches, songs, and a video — it's going to be amazing!"

There was silence for a few moments. Mr. and Mrs. Gerstein were both speechless, very moved by the news. After regaining his composure, Mr. Gerstein spoke. "Yaakov, I'm sure that I speak for

Mommy when I say that we are very touched by what you've told us. We are truly blessed to have such wonderful children. But I'd like to ask you to hold off on renting the hall and hiring the caterer until Mommy and I discuss it. We'll get back to you in a day or so."

The following night, Mr. Gerstein called Yaakov and said that they wanted to make a conference call that night with all the children and their spouses. At eight o'clock, everyone called in and Mr. Gerstein began:

"Children, Mommy and I are so touched by what you're planning. We're so grateful, to Hashem and to you. But Mommy and I understand that such a celebration will cost thousands of dollars. For a wedding, that's what it costs, but we don't think we want you spending thousands of dollars for an anniversary party. So here's what we suggest. Let's have an anniversary party just for children and grandchildren in one of our homes. If no home is big enough, then we can find a shul basement that's not expensive. As far as the food, let's have it homemade, like we do for our Chanukah *mesibah*.

"And if you children really want to spend all that money, then here's our suggestion: Figure out how much the grand catered celebration would have cost and give that money to Mommy and me so that we can give it out to various *tzedakah* causes.

"That would be a great anniversary present!"

The Gift of Life

"And now, honored with the fourth *berachah,* Mr. Chaim Feldstein."*

"Who is that? He's not related... I know both families. Why did they give him a berachah under the chuppah?"

"He's the one who donated a kidney to the chassan's father."

"Oh, now I understand."

Mr. Feldstein had donated a kidney to save the life of the

chassan's father. Only Hashem can repay Mr. Feldstein for his amazing act of *chesed.* But the *chassan's* father wanted to express his appreciation to Mr. Feldstein in some way. He found the opportunity when his son got married. It is an honor to be called to the *chuppah* to recite one of the *sheva berachos.* These honors are usually given to rabbanim, roshei yeshivah, grandfathers, and other close relatives. Mr. Feldstein was given one of these honors as a small token of appreciation.

Sometimes, a child might be upset over something that his parents asked him to do, or something that they will not allow him to do, and the child might be upset to the point that he wants to say something disrespectful. At such times, says Rav Nissim Karelitz (a great *posek* in Eretz Yisrael), the child should tell himself:

"Would I speak disrespectfully to someone who saved my life? Of course not! Even if I were upset about something he did, I could never bring myself to speak to him with anything but respect.

"Well, my parents *gave me life.* They brought me into this world and have taken care of me since the moment I was born. There is no way I can ever repay them for all that they have done for me. *And* the Torah commands me to honor and respect them. When I honor them, Hashem considers it as if I honored Him. And when I show them disrespect, it is as if I have shown Him disrespect.

"I have no choice but to remain respectful even if I'm upset."

Chapter Three
Exceptional Honor

Kibbud Av VaEim Brings Miracles

It was a difficult time for the Jewish people. Moshe Rabbeinu had passed away, his *talmid* and successor Yehoshua bin Nun had passed away, and the Jews' enemies were attacking them. The Midyanim, in particular, were wreaking havoc on Jewish land, destroying crops and stealing livestock.

It had gotten so bad that people were afraid to thresh (separate the wheat kernels from the husks) on the threshing floor. Instead, they would do it secretly at the wine press, hoping that the Midyanim wouldn't discover them!

One night, Yoash, a leader of his town in Shevet Menashe's territory, was threshing his grain at his wine press. His son Gidon said to him, "Father, I am afraid that the Midyanim might launch a surprise attack and it will be hard for you to run away. Please return to our house, and I will do the threshing for you."

At that moment, Hashem said, "You have fulfilled the mitzvah of *kibbud av.* Surely, you are deserving that the Jews should be saved through you." Gidon would become the next *shofet* of the Jewish people and lead them to victory over their enemies.

In the following story, we see how *kibbud av va'eim* saved lives.

A Bar Mitzvah to Remember

"How can we make the bar mitzvah without him?"

"We can't. We have no choice. We'll have to change our plans."

It was the month of Adar 5698 (1938). Reb Shmaya and Mrs. Rivkah Reichman of Vienna, Austria, were preparing to celebrate the bar mitzvah of their oldest son, Eli. The plan was to have Eli called to the Torah on Shabbos morning in the Adas Yisrael shul where they *davened,* and then to hold a *melaveh malkah* celebration on Motza'ei Shabbos.

But a few days earlier, they had received the news that Eli's grandfather Reb Dovid Reichman had suffered a stroke and was too weak to travel from his home in Beled, Hungary. If the bar mitzvah took place as planned, he would not be able to attend.

What should they do?

To Reb Shmaya and his devoted wife, there was only one solution.

"If Zeidy cannot come to the bar mitzvah, then we will bring the bar mitzvah to him. We'll cancel our plans here in Vienna and celebrate with a small crowd in Beled. But Zeidy will be there, and that is what's most important."

They were not able to take their younger children along. Reb Shmaya, his wife, and the older children arrived in Beled on Erev Shabbos and began to prepare for a special Shabbos with Zeidy and Bubby Reichman.

On Friday night, as they were eating the *seudas Shabbos,* they heard shouting in the street but tried to ignore it. They had come to celebrate and did not want anything to mar their joy.

On Motza'ei Shabbos, as they were preparing for the *melaveh malkah,* they found out that the shouting had come from non-Jews who were celebrating something terrible. On that Friday night, March 12, 1938, German troops had marched into Vienna

The great baal tzedakah Reb Moshe Reichman was a son of Reb Shmaya and Mrs. Rivkah Reichman, whose lives were saved because of their kibbud av va'eim.

as Germany officially annexed Austria, making it part of the German empire. This was to become known as the *Anschluss* (Annexation) and was another step that Hitler, *ym"s,* the wicked leader of Germany, had taken toward his twin goals of conquering the world and ridding it of its Jews, *chas v'shalom.*

That Friday night, Nazi soldiers entered Jewish neighborhoods in Vienna where they beat Jewish men, smashed Jewish store windows, and set some buildings on fire.

They also searched for Reb Shmaya Reichman, whom they knew was a wealthy businessman.

They could not find him because he had gone to Beled, Hungary, so that his elderly, ill father could participate in his son's bar mitzvah.

The Reichmans were reunited with the rest of their children, but Reb Shmaya never returned to Vienna. Eventually, he would settle in Toronto, Ontario, where he and his children were known as exceptionally fine, generous people who were always ready to help another Jew. One of his sons, Reb Moshe, was to become one of the greatest *baalei tzedakah* the world has ever known.

And all of this was possible because Reb Shmaya and his wife could not celebrate their son Eli's bar mitzvah without Eli's zeide being there.

Kibbud av had saved Reb Shmaya's life.

For the Sake of His Learning

"A person must have a very great *zechus* to marry a *gadol hador.* How did the Rebbetzin merit to marry her husband?"

This question was asked to Rebbetzin Batsheva Kanievsky, wife of the prince of Torah in our generation, Rabbi Chaim Kanievsky. No one can claim to know the answer to this question for sure, but Rebbetzin Kanievsky offered a possible answer.

"When I was young, I honored my father (Rabbi Yosef Shalom Elyashiv) very much under difficult circumstances.

"It happened during the Israeli War of Independence in 1948. There were severe food shortages; people had to stand in line for hours to buy bread and other basic foods. My father would stand in line every day to get food for our family. My father learned Torah every free moment, from early morning until late at night.

Walking from the home of her grandparents, Rabbi and Rebbetzin Aryeh Levin, was dangerous, but Rebbetzin Kanievsky did it for the sake of her father's learning.

Having to stand on line every day took away much precious time from his learning.

"One day, I said to him, 'Abba, from now on, I'll take care of getting food so you can learn without being disturbed.'

"At that time, we were not living at home in Meah Shearim because our home was too close to the war zone. We were living temporarily in the Mishkenot neighborhood with my mother's parents, Rav and Rebbetzin Aryeh Levin. But to get our daily food rations, I had to walk to Meah Shearim where our apartment was, because food was given out in each neighborhood only for residents of that neighborhood. And we were visitors to the Mishkenot neighborhood, not residents.

"It was very dangerous during wartime for me, a young girl, to walk every day from Mishkenot to Meah Shearim to stand on line for food. But I did it so that my father could learn our holy Torah without interruption.

"Perhaps that is why Hashem granted me such a special husband who, like my father, never stops learning."

A Drive That Was Well Worth It

Rabbi Meir Zlotowitz was a very busy person. He was the founder and president of ArtScroll Publications, the world's largest publisher of Jewish *sefarim* and books for the English reader. He was usually at his desk from early morning until late in the evening — when he wasn't traveling to Eretz Yisrael or other places to meet with *gedolei Yisrael* and other important people.

As busy as he was, his family was always on his mind. As long as his father and mother were alive, Rabbi Zlotowitz did whatever he could for them.

Some days, he would be driving somewhere and the GPS or Waze route, which is the fastest way between two points, would take him past his parents' house — but he purposely would not

Rabbi Meir Zlotowitz was a very busy person, but never too busy to help his parents.

go that way! "Right now I'm in a big hurry to make an appointment," he would explain, "and I don't have time to stop in and visit my parents. But I don't feel right passing by their house and not stopping in to at least say hello. So I'll go a different way."

One year, Rabbi Zlotowitz and his wife and children were planning to spend Pesach at a hotel in the Catskill Mountains. He invited his parents to join them and was disappointed when they declined the invitation without giving any explanation. Rabbi Zlotowitz wondered, "Why don't they want to join us? It would be so wonderful for them to be with their children and grandchildren around the Seder table in a nice hotel with fresh country air." The more he thought about it, the more Rabbi Zlotowitz was convinced that he knew why his parents didn't want to come.

His father was very, very careful that everything he ate was one hundred percent kosher. On Pesach, we have to be even more careful than usual with what we eat because we have to be sure that everything is "kosher for Pesach." Rabbi Zlotowitz guessed correctly that his father was afraid that perhaps in the kitchen at the hotel they were not as careful as he would be at home.

Rabbi Zlotowitz had an idea. One day shortly before Pesach he asked his father, "Daddy, it's a beautiful day. How would you like to take a drive with me to the Catskill Mountains?" Rabbi Aharon Zlotowitz always enjoyed spending time with his son. Soon they were in Rabbi Meir's car on the way to the Catskills.

After a couple of hours, they arrived at the hotel. Rabbi Zlotowitz escorted his father into the kitchen where the Pesach food was being prepared. Rabbi Aharon Zlotowitz saw how careful the cook was to keep everything *kosher l'Pesach* and also how the *mashgiach* of the kitchen was making sure that everything was being done correctly.

When they left the hotel, Rabbi Aharon Zlotowitz said to his son, "We can eat the food from this kitchen." And to Rabbi Meir Zlotowitz's great joy, his parents were now happy to join his family at the hotel for Pesach.

> *Rabbi Meir Zlotowitz was a very busy person, and driving his father to the hotel took up most of a day — time he could have used to accomplish a lot as president of ArtScroll Publications. He believed — as all of us have to believe — that we never lose out from doing a mitzvah, especially a mitzvah as precious as kibbud av va'eim.*

Gut Voch and Goodbye

"No, we have to go back."

"Are you sure? We're already on the road half an hour. If we go back, we'll lose an hour in total."

"I realize that. We have to go back."

Rabbi Aharon Aryeh Leib Kalmanowitz was a famous Rav in Lithuania who was often asked to be part of a *beis din* when difficult cases had to be decided. One Motza'ei Shabbos, he received an urgent message asking that he come immediately to be part of a *beis din.* He had left in a rush; only after he was well on his way did he realize something. "Oh, no! I left town without wishing my parents *a gut voch*. I always do that. I must go back."

And so he told the driver to turn the wagon around and head back to town. Wishing his parents *a gut voch* was too important to miss, even if it meant that his trip would take much longer.

Another time, Rav Kalmanowitz returned home toward the end of a harsh winter after being away for six months.

"Aharon," his rebbetzin said after he had spent some time with her and their children, "you are surely exhausted from the journey home in such deep snow. Please go rest while I prepare a hot meal."

"My dear wife, there is one thing that I want right now, and that is to visit my parents, whom I have also not seen these past six months. Would it be all right if I go visit them now?"

"Aharon, you know that I would never stop you from visiting your parents. But are you sure you have the strength for it? After all, they live a few miles away and all the wagon drivers have closed up shop until the snow stops falling!"

"That's all right. I'll borrow a pair of high boots and walk."

And that is what he did.

◆ ◆ ◆

Imagine that you are vacationing in Florida and your mother in New York will soon be traveling to Eretz Yisrael. Of course, you want to say goodbye to her and wish her a safe and successful trip. How would you do that?

"That's simple!" you might think. "I'd pick up the phone and call my mother. How else should I say goodbye when I'm so far away?"

Well, let me introduce you to Reb Yitzchak HaKohen Wallerstein.

Reb Yitzchak was what people call a "simple Jew" who lived in Monsey, New York. In truth, he wasn't simple; he was really exceptional. For example, he excelled in the mitzvah of *kibbud av va'eim*.

He would drive from Monsey to Manhattan every Friday so that he could wish his mother good Shabbos in person (his father had already passed away) and get a *berachah* from her.

Reb Yitzchak was not wealthy, but whenever his mother traveled to Eretz Yisrael, he would buy her a first-class ticket, which is very expensive but allowed her to travel in comfort.

Once, Reb Yitzchak was vacationing in Florida when his mother was preparing to leave to Eretz Yisrael from Kennedy Airport in New York. Reb Yitzchak flew to Kennedy Airport, wished his mother a safe trip, asked for her *berachah* and received it, and headed right back to Florida.

No, he certainly was not a "simple Jew."

To Bring Them Joy

Over the course of his life, Rabbi Yaakov Yisrael Kanievsky, the Steipler Gaon, published many volumes of his *sefer Kehillos Yaakov* on Gemara. The final volume was published during his last years when he was ill and weak.

Over the years, he received many letters from *talmidei chachamim* who had learned his *sefarim* and had questions about something he had written. It gives any author, especially a *talmid chacham* who writes *divrei Torah,* pleasure to know that people are reading what he wrote and are even taking the time to write a letter about it. The Steipler was very pleased when he received such letters. And of course, he would write back.

One day, after a while had passed since his final *sefer* was published, the Steipler told his son Rabbi Chaim Kanievsky with sadness, "I haven't received even one letter about my new *sefer.* It looks like no one is learning it."

Seeing his father's distress, Rav Chaim approached a *talmid chacham* and asked that he learn part of his father's new *sefer* and write a comment or question to him. Rav Chaim cautioned him that, of course, his father should not know that he had spoken to him.

The letter that Rav Chaim arranged brought his father much joy.

A short while later, the Steipler happily told his son that he had received a letter about something he had written in his new *sefer*.

Rabbi Yosef Reuven Gershonowitz was a renowned *talmid chacham* who lived in Eretz Yisrael. When his father passed away, his mother came to live with him and his family.

Rav Yosef Reuven and his wife treated his mother royally. Rav Yosef Reuven gave up his own bed for his mother; for the rest of her life, he slept in an armchair.

His mother was supposed to receive a monthly check from a certain organization. At some point, the checks stopped coming, and Rav Yosef Reuven's mother was very upset. Rav Yosef Reuven came up with a plan to eliminate her distress.

Each month, he would take a large portion of his own salary, put it into an envelope, and write the organization's name as the return address. When the first such envelope arrived in the mail, his mother was very happy that she was once again receiving her monthly payments. She gave most of the money to Rav Yosef Reuven, since he was providing her with room and board, and donated the rest of the money to *tzedakah*.

Rav Yosef Reuven had a brother who lived overseas. His mother was very happy and excited whenever she got a letter from him. (In those days, overseas phone calls were very expensive; most families kept in touch with overseas relatives only by mail.) Rav Yosef Reuven would visit his city's central post office every week to see if a letter from his brother might have come. He could have just waited for the mailman to deliver it to his apartment, but knowing how much these letters meant to his mother, he wanted her to receive them as soon as possible.

Finding the Right Chair

Only a couple of days before Rosh Hashanah, Shlomie Gross, a beloved Flatbush resident and *baal tzedakah,* was in a local shul. There was no one else in the shul, but had there been, he surely would have wondered about this strange sight. Shlomie was in the women's section, sitting in a chair for a few moments, then sitting on a different chair, and then another.

The reason for his actions soon became clear when he got in touch with the shul's *gabbai.* Shlomie's mother was planning to *daven* in that shul on Rosh Hashanah. Knowing that the women's section had an assortment of chairs, Shlomie had come to try out the different chairs so that he could find the one that his mother would find most comfortable. When he did, he asked the *gabbai* to reserve that chair for his mother.

Once, Shlomie's mother was planning to fly overseas alone. (Her husband had passed away by that time.) Shlomie arranged for her to fly in the first-class section so that she could be as comfortable as possible — but that was not all. He drove his mother to the airport. In the airport, he approached a *frum* young man who was going to be on the same flight but had a coach ticket, for a seat in the less expensive section of the plane.

"I want to make you an offer," said Shlomie. "My mother is going to be flying first class. I'll pay to have your ticket upgraded to first class so that you'll sit not far from my mother. I would like you to keep an eye on my mother and make sure that she has whatever she needs throughout the flight." The young man was happy to oblige, and the "deal" was made.

A "Deal" With the Rain

"Of course I respect our Rav! But what can we do? His eyesight is failing, so he can't prepare *shiurim*. I think we have to ask him to retire."

For over forty years, Rabbi Shmuel Follman was a very respected and beloved Rav in a Tel Aviv shul. His most important *shiur* of the week, given on Shabbos afternoon, began with Gemara and ended with beautiful thoughts on the weekly *parashah*. Now, he could no longer give that *shiur* — or any other. He could barely see.

Rav Shmuel's son was Rabbi Ben Zion Follman of Bnei Brak, a very beloved *rosh kollel.* When Rav Ben Zion found out that his father was going to be asked to retire, he was extremely upset. He knew that his father, even without his vision, could still accomplish a lot as a Rav. He also knew that both his father and his mother would be very hurt if his father was forced into retirement.

Rav Ben Zion thought of a solution. He called up the shul's *gabbai* and said, "Please do not say anything to my father. Allow him to remain as your Rav. As far as his Shabbos afternoon *shiur,* which is his main *shiur* of the week, don't worry. I'll give the *shiur* each week."

"*You'll* give the *shiur*?" the *gabbai* asked in shock. "But it takes an hour and twenty minutes to walk from Bnei Brak to our shul in Tel Aviv. You're going to walk so far *every single week*?"

"Yes," Rav Ben Zion replied, "every single week."

For the next fifteen years Rav Ben Zion walked for an hour and twenty minutes to Tel Aviv on Shabbos afternoon so that he could substitute for his father at his weekly *shiur.*

Rav Ben Zion's mother was grateful to him, but she was worried. "What will happen if you get caught in a downpour on the way?" she asked him. "It's Shabbos and you can't carry an umbrella."

"Do not worry, Mama," Rav Ben Zion assured his mother. "I have a 'deal' with the rain — it always waits until I arrive at the shul!"

For a very long time, it never rained during his walks to Tel Aviv. One day, Rav Ben Zion told some of his *talmidim*, "I am so grateful to Hashem. I walk to Tel Aviv every Shabbos and not once has it rained."

The next Shabbos it poured as he was walking. Rav Ben Zion thought about what had happened. He felt that it was not a coincidence that it poured *only* on the week when he had spoken about it not raining. The Gemara teaches that there is more *berachah* when things are kept quiet, out of the public view. He decided that never again would he speak about his weekly "miracle."

And for the rest of those fifteen years, it never again rained during his Shabbos walk.

For fifteen years, Rav Ben Zion walked a great distance each Shabbos for the sake of his father.

A Present for His Mother

What would you do with the hard-earned sum of eighty-four dollars?

Shaya Alpert, a young teenager, knew exactly what he wanted to do with it.

He earned that money one Erev Pesach. Shaya lived in a high-rise apartment building on New York's Lower East Side. Many of the building's residents were elderly, and it was very difficult for them to go outside to the street to burn their *chametz*. Shaya would knock on the doors of the Jewish residents and offer to burn their *chametz* for them. He never asked for money, but if someone gave him a tip, he accepted it. One time, he tried to refuse the tip, but the person was insistent, so in the end, Shaya accepted it.

That person was the leader of the generation, Rabbi Moshe Feinstein. Shaya's father, Rabbi Nisson Alpert, was a close *talmid* of Rav Moshe and like a son to him. Shaya too was very close to Rav Moshe. Once, when Rebbetzin Feinstein was hospitalized, Shaya was asked to spend the night in Rav Moshe's apartment so that he would not be alone.

So when Rav Moshe gave Shaya his *chametz* along with a five-dollar bill, Shaya did not want to accept the money. But he had no choice when Rav Moshe told him, "If you don't take the money, I will not let you burn my *chametz*!"

One Erev Pesach after completing his rounds and burning the *chametz,* Shaya went upstairs to his family's apartment. He rang the bell and his mother came to the door. "Mommy," he said, "I don't want to come inside because I smell from the smoke of the fire. Could you please bring me a clean shirt and I'll change here?"

He then handed his mother an envelope that held the eighty-four dollars he had earned that morning. "Mommy, this is for you. Please buy yourself a dress for Yom Tov."

Shaya wanted to burn Rav Moshe's chametz for free, but Rav Moshe insisted on paying.

Shaya's mother was speechless. But in her heart, she thanked Hashem for granting her such a special son.

Not every child has such a sum of money to give his father or mother, but there are other ways for a child to show appreciation to a parent for all that they do for him. It can be a small gift, a short note, or some other nice surprise. Parents appreciate when they are appreciated.

The Best Bid

"Will everyone please find his seat! The bidding will begin momentarily..."

It was Simchas Torah morning at Congregation Anshei Achdus.* Shacharis had just ended, and *hakafos* would soon begin. As was done every year, before *hakafos* the *gabbai* sold *aliyos* to the highest bidder. This included *Kol HaNe'arim,* the *aliyah* when all the young children are called up together to the Torah; and *Maftir,* which on Simchas Torah is usually sold for quite a large sum.

The two most special *aliyos, Chassan Torah,* when the last

parashah of the Torah is completed, and *Chassan Bereishis,* when we begin the Torah once again, were not sold. *Chassan Torah* was always given to the Rav, and *Chassan Bereishis* was given to Reb Dovid,* an elderly *talmid chacham* who had been *davening* in the shul since he was a young man.

"Now listen carefully..." the *gabbai* continued, to everyone's surprise. What was he going to say? Everyone knew how the bidding worked.

"This year, since the shul is badly in need of funds, we have decided to sell *Chassan Bereishis* to the highest bidder. I've spoken to Reb Dovid and he is fine with it. So let's begin the bidding by selling *Chassan Bereishis.*"

People were excited. It had been many years since *Chassan Berei-shis* was sold. Reb Dovid seemed very calm. He was a humble man and was probably happy to help the shul by giving up his annual *zechus.*

One person, however, was not happy at all — Reb Dovid's devoted son, Reuven.*

"It's not right," he thought to himself. "Aside from the Rav, there is no one in our shul who can match my father's Torah knowledge. When the Rav is away, my father is always the one who fills in and gives the *shiurim.* How can they take this *kibbud* (honor) away from him?"

Reuven was upset, but he was not about to start an argument. That would certainly not bring honor to his father. As he sat lost in thought, he heard the bidding begin.

"Five hundred dollars for *Chassan Bereishis...* five hundred dollars... five hundred dollars going once..."

Reuven looked around, trying to figure out who had made the bid. It didn't take long. Mr. Bandman,* the richest member of the shul, was smiling, as were his sons and grandsons. He had made the bid.

"I wish I could buy the *aliyah* for my father," Reuven thought.

"But there's no way that I, a simple manager in a local clothing store, can outbid Mr. Bandman.

"...But wait! I can at least try. Worst comes to worst, I'll borrow some money from a *gemach* and pay it back in monthly installments."

"Six hundred dollars!" Reuven shouted.

All heads, including Mr. Bandman's, turned in Reuven's direction. Was he serious? Was he getting into a bidding war with the shul's richest member?

"Seven hundred," Mr. Bandman called out.

"Eight hundred," Reuven responded.

"Nine hundred," Mr. Bandman announced. When the bidding had started he was smiling. Now, he looked quite serious. The atmosphere in the shul was tense. No one had expected a bidding war between the shul's richest man and someone who barely made a living.

Reuven also looked serious, and though he didn't show it, he was nervous. For him, this was a lot of money. But he was determined to get that *aliyah* for his father.

"One thousand," Reuven announced. You could hear people gasp. They couldn't believe what was happening.

Mr. Bandman turned to his sons. "I could go much higher, but I see that Reuven wants the *aliyah* very badly. He's probably buying it for his father. I think I'll stop here."

Reb Dovid was called to the Torah for *Chassan Bereishis* and everyone, including Mr. Bandman, was happy for him — and for his wonderful son who beamed with pride and pleasure as he watched his father ascend the *bimah*. "Paying this pledge is not going to be easy," he thought, "but I have no regrets."

Shortly after this incident, Reuven decided to take a bit of money he had saved up and use it to start a spice factory. His new business did very well and within a short time, he was wealthy. Paying the pledge was not difficult at all.

Reuven was already looking forward to the next Simchas Torah...

Certificate of Honor

In the 1990s, Rabbi Yitzy Bald was very close to receiving *semichah* from his rebbi, Rabbi Avraham Pam. To receive *semichah,* a *ben Torah* must study some very difficult parts of *Shulchan Aruch* and be tested on them. If he passes all the *bechinos* (tests), then he receives *semichah*. The Rav who tested him signs a certificate that says that the person has passed his tests in these halachos and can be considered an expert in them. Someone who receives *semichah* earns the title "Rabbi."

At the time of our story, "Yitzy" had passed four of five required *bechinos*. But with his mother seriously ill, he didn't think that he had the time, or the peace of mind, to master the remaining halachos needed for *semichah*. He decided to put his study for *semichah* on hold.

One day, Yitzy's mother asked, "What's with your *semichah*? Do you think that you'll be receiving *semichah* soon?" Yitzy did not give his mother a clear answer. "Oh, no," he said to himself, "I didn't realize how important it is to Ima that I receive my *semichah* and be called 'Rabbi.'

"Well, obviously it's important to her. I guess I'll just have to put my mind to it and study as hard as I can."

He and his *chavrusa* resumed learning the halachos; before long, they were tested by Rav Pam, who was satisfied with their knowledge. They would be receiving *semichah*!

This happened shortly before Pesach. Rav Pam's *semichah* certificates were written in his beautiful handwriting and took him a long time to write. During the school year when he was busy teaching Torah, it was hard for him to find the time to write *semichah* certificates. That's why he would write them in the summer when yeshivah was closed.

For the sake of Yitzy's mother, Rav Pam found the time to write his semichah certificate.

A few days after Yitzy passed his last *bechinah,* his mother asked, "Yitzy, when will you be receiving your *semichah* certificate? I would love to see it."

On the Friday morning before Pesach, Yitzy called Rav Pam. "I really feel bad bothering Rebbi, especially right before Pesach when everyone is so busy. But my mother, who as Rebbi knows is not well, mentioned that she would love to see my *semichah* certificate. Is it possible that Rebbi could find some time after Pesach to write it?"

"Call me back in a few days," said Rav Pam.

A friend of Yitzy had given him a beeper to wear so that his mother could reach him immediately if necessary. That same Friday afternoon, as Yitzy was shopping for Shabbos, the beeper vibrated. His mother was trying to reach him.

In those days, when cellphones were not yet common, Yitzy had to run to the nearest pay phone on the street to call his mother. "Yitzy," his mother said excitedly, "Rav Pam called — your *semichah* is ready! Rav Pam said that you can pick it up this afternoon!"

An hour before Shabbos, Yitzy rang his rebbi's doorbell. Rav Pam handed him the certificate and Yitzy said, "Rebbi, this means so much to my mother. I can't thank Rebbi enough."

Ram Pam responded by giving his dear *talmid* a hug. To this day, Rabbi Yitzy Bald is moved every time he thinks of what his rebbi did to make his mother happy.

Time Well Spent

Asher Tepler* lived in New Jersey, while his mother lived in New York, in the house in which Asher and his siblings had grown up. All the children were married and Asher's father had passed away. Mrs. Tepler enjoyed her children and grandchildren, but it was not always easy living alone.

On Chanukah, the entire family came to Mrs. Tepler for a beautiful Chanukah party, featuring lively singing, a story told by one of Asher's brothers, and of course, Bubby Tepler's delicious potato latkes. By late afternoon, everyone had left, heading home to light the menorah.

The next night, Asher called his mother. "Mom, I want to thank you for having everyone over yesterday. It's so wonderful when the whole family gets together."

"I know, Asher, I'm so blessed. But I have to tell you the truth: After everyone left, I got this sad feeling. It's hard when everyone leaves and I'm by myself."

Asher felt very bad. He understood his mother's feelings. "Mom, would you like me to come over now and visit? I could be there in around an hour."

"Asher, that's so sweet of you. But no, it's okay. Actually, I wasn't supposed to be home tonight. One of my neighbors is making a wedding in Lakewood, and I really wanted to go. But I couldn't find a ride."

"Mom," Asher replied with excitement, "you *do* have a ride. I'm leaving my house right now to come pick you up and take you to the wedding. You'll probably miss the *chuppah*, but we should arrive for the beginning of the meal. When we get there,

I'll try to find you a ride back to Brooklyn toward the end of the wedding. If I can't find a ride, I'll be happy to wait to drive you back."

Mrs. Tepler tried to talk her son out of his grand plan, but he was determined to follow through. An hour later, he was helping his mother into the car.

"Asher," his mother said, "I knew before tonight that I was blessed. But now I have even more reason to be grateful to Hashem for giving me such wonderful children."

"Mom, it's really my pleasure. I can't think of a better way to spend my evening."

"And the Winner Is..."

"I'm ready to give it."

"So am I."

"I would be happy to do so."

"I would also like the *zechus*..."

Rabbi Avraham Ravitz was a famous *talmid chacham* and a respected member of the United Torah Judaism party in the Israeli Knesset. He drew people closer to Torah and dedicated his life to *Klal Yisrael.*

When he suffered kidney failure, the doctors said that he had to have a kidney transplant to save his life.

By that time, all of Rabbi Ravitz's twelve children were adults. Each one of them wanted the *zechus* of donating the kidney that would save their father's life.

But donating a kidney is not that simple. To be a donor, one must be a "match" with the recipient, the one who needs the kidney. Not only do the blood types of the two people have to match, there are other factors that doctors must check before they can decide if Mr. X can donate a kidney to Mr. Y.

After all the tests were run, two of Rabbi Ravitz's children were found to be the best matches for their father.

Both wanted to be the one to give his kidney. This would mean undergoing surgery to remove the kidney and then having to recover from the surgery. This did not worry either of them. What wouldn't a son do for his father?

They went to the *gadol hador,* Rabbi Yosef Shalom Elyashiv, to ask him who should be the one to give the kidney. Rav Elyashiv said that he would cast the *Goral HaGra.* (The *Goral HaGra* is a method taught by the Vilna Gaon, known as the Gra [גָּאוֹן רַבֵּינוּ אֱלִיָּהוּ], to find the answer to very important questions. It is done by turning the pages of a certain type of *Tanach* in a very specific order. When a person follows this method, he will find the answer to his question in a *pasuk* on the page that he turns to at the very end.)

The *goral* was cast and a *pasuk* clearly indicated the name of one of the two sons. He donated one of his kidneys and the surgery was performed.

This story became a news sensation in Eretz Yisrael. All the newspapers, even those published by non-religious Jews, wrote

Rav Elyashiv said that he would cast the Goral HaGra.

about how this Jew's life had been saved after his twelve children volunteered to donate a kidney, and how Rav Elyashiv solved the problem through the *Goral HaGra.*

Rachamim,* an elderly Jew living in Tel Aviv, read these newspaper articles. He was amazed and very sad at the same time. Rachamim was not religious. He had two grown children, a son and a daughter. A few years earlier, his kidneys had failed and he needed a transplant. Both of his children were matches, but neither wanted to donate a kidney to save their father's life.

His son said, "I already made plans to travel overseas; I can't let a surgery delay my plans."

His daughter said, "The new college term is beginning soon. If I have surgery, it will ruin the beginning of the term."

Eventually, a donor was found and Rachamim's life was saved. But every time he thought about his children's attitude, it made him sad.

> *I gave my children their very lives. I was so devoted to them, I spent all my money on them, I sent them to excellent schools, I nurtured them and made sure that they had whatever they needed — yet, they were too busy with their own lives to come to my rescue when my life was in danger.*

Rachamim read the story about Rabbi Ravitz and how his twelve children were "fighting" over who would be lucky enough to help him. Rachamim said to himself, "The Torah must be very special that it could make children be so devoted to their parents. What a shame that I never studied Torah or fulfilled its mitzvos.

"But it's not too late. I will start keeping mitzvos now and will continue until the end of my life."

And that is how Rachamim became a *baal teshuvah.* His story became known when he started attending *minyan* daily and told the members of his shul why he had started coming. The *kibbud av* of Rabbi Ravitz's children had led this man to attach himself to Hashem and His Torah.

An Honored Escort

"Oh, I am sooo hungry!" Yehudah* thought to himself. "It's a shame I woke up late and had to *daven* at a late *minyan*. After *davening*, I just had time to eat one cookie — and now it's almost one o'clock and I'm feeling weak. It's going to be hard for me to concentrate on Rebbi's Gemara *shiur*. What a shame — I *love* his *shiur*!"

This story happened around 150 years ago. Yehudah was an orphaned teenage boy and his rebbi was Rabbi Yaakov Yitzchak of Peshischa, a chassidic leader known as the Yid HaKadosh (the Holy Jew). He was a brilliant *talmid chacham* whose *shiurim* were very deep. This meant that the *talmidim* had to concentrate a lot on what he was saying, and that is why it was especially hard for Yehudah that day.

In the middle of that *shiur* something very unusual happened. Rav Yaakov Yitzchak suddenly thought of a question on the Gemara he was teaching. As the *talmidim* waited patiently in silence, their rebbi sat with his eyes closed for a long time, deep in thought, as he tried to think of an answer to his question. This happened occasionally. Rav Yaakov Yitzchak could sometimes think in silence for a half-hour.

Meanwhile, Yehudah was feeling weaker and hungrier by the minute. Finally, he thought, "Rebbi has been thinking quietly for a while, and he might be doing so for much longer. It's a perfect time for me to run home and eat something!"

He closed his gemara and quietly left the room. He ran home as fast as he could, grabbed a snack and ate it very quickly, said a *berachah acharonah,* and was already by the front door when he heard his mother calling him.

"Yehudah," she said, "it's so good that you came home just now! I need something from the attic, and you know how hard it is for me to climb up there. Could you please get it for me?"

"Mama," Yehudah replied, "I'm so sorry, but I'm in a hurry to get back for the *shiur*. Would it be okay if I went up to the attic later, after the *shiur* is over?"

"It's okay, Yehudah," his mother said. "I really need that thing right now, but I know that the *shiur* is important to you. Go back; I can go up to the attic myself."

Yehudah thanked his mother and closed the front door behind him. But then he stopped and asked himself, "Is that the right way? An opportunity for *kibbud eim* has presented itself and I'm going to ignore my mother's request?"

Quickly, he turned around, went up to the attic, and brought the item to his mother. From the look of appreciation on her face, it was obvious to Yehudah that he had done the right thing. Quickly, he hurried back to the *shiur,* hoping that he hadn't missed too much.

As Yehudah entered the beis midrash, the Yid HaKadosh looked at him, then rose from his chair and asked him, "Tell me, what mitzvah did you just perform?"

Yehudah was not comfortable announcing in front of all his friends how he had gone home for a snack and ended up helping his mother. But his rebbi had asked him a question and he had to answer it. He proceeded to relate all that had happened from the moment he left the beis midrash until the moment he returned.

When Yehudah finished, the Yid HaKadosh said, "When you entered the beis midrash, I saw that you were accompanied by the *neshamah* of the great Abaye [who is mentioned in the Gemara throughout *Shas*]. Until you returned to the beis midrash, I had not thought of an answer to my *kasha.* But in Abaye's *zechus,* I have now thought of a wonderful answer.

"You see, Abaye was orphaned from both his father and mother as an infant. In fact, the letters of his name, אַבַּיֵי, are the initials of אֲשֶׁר בְּךָ יְרֻחַם יָתוֹם (*For it is with You that an orphan finds mercy* — *Hoshea* 14:4). Because he never knew his own parents, Abaye's *neshamah* accompanies those who honor their parents, so that he can have a share in their mitzvah. And that is how I was able to answer my question."

The Champion

When Mr. Shaul Tzvi Zeisler's father passed away, a non-Jewish neighbor came to the *shivah* house. Before Mr. Zeisler could say anything, the visitor blurted out, "You are a champion!" He explained:

> *I live directly across the street. I'm retired and I don't have to get up at 5:30 in the morning. But a number of years ago, I was up early one morning and I saw how you came to your father's home to take him to the synagogue. I watched how you held his hand gently and helped him down the front stairs. I watched how you walked him to your car. I could not get over how you treated him with such dignity.*
>
> *I got up the next morning and watched again how you treated him with loving care. No one in my community does this. I made it a point to get up early every morning just to watch how you took care of your father — such loving care! That daily scene carried me through the entire day.*

The man became emotional as he concluded, "But now that he died, where I am going to get my inspiration? What am I going to do now?"

The man burst into tears and quickly left the house.

I sometimes *daven* Minchah in a shul where one of the regular *mispallelim* is a man in his nineties who cannot walk without assistance. Every day he is escorted to shul by his daughter or a grandchild, and every day when Minchah ends, his daughter or grandchild is waiting to walk him home. He is always greeted with a smile, a smile that says, "Tatty (or Zeidy), it is such a pleasure, such a *zechus,* to be able to assist you."

How fortunate we are to be a part of the *Am Nivchar,* the Chosen People, who live by Hashem's mitzvos, as taught to us by our dear parents.

Chapter Four
Even When It's Hard

No Excuses

Kibbud av va'eim is a very important mitzvah, but not necessarily an easy one. Sometimes, our parents want us to do something for them when we would rather be doing something else. For example, a mother might ask her daughter to set the table when she would rather be outside playing with friends.

Sometimes, our parents want us to do a chore that we find difficult — a father might ask his son to help him clean up the yard, which is full of leaves and litter.

From the great Rosh Yeshivah of Yeshivas Mir Yerushalayim, Rabbi Nosson Tzvi Finkel, we can learn that there are no excuses. *Kibbud av va'eim* is a mitzvah that we should want to do even when it's difficult.

When he was a young man in his thirties, Rav Nosson Tzvi was stricken with Parkinson's disease, a terrible illness that makes a person weak, causes pain, and affects the nervous system.

Rav Nosson Tzvi's mother, Rebbetzin Sarah Finkel, outlived him by some ten years. (She recently passed away at age 100.) I

Even when he was stricken with Parkinson's, Rav Nosson Tzvi continued to climb the steps to visit his mother.

had the *zechus* to know her; I visited her at her home in Yerushalayim a couple of times and we communicated often through email. Once, I wrote to her that I was writing a book about *kibbud av va'eim*[2] and asked if she could tell me about how her son Rav Nosson Tzvi fulfilled this mitzvah. This is what she replied:

> *My two sons [Rebbetzin Finkel had two children, Rav Nosson Tzvi and* יבל״ח *Rav Gedaliah] have always been very makpid (careful) about the mitzvah of kibbud av va'eim. As busy as my late son Rav Nosson Zvi zt"l was, he always made it a point to join me for breakfast each Friday morning before he gave his Friday morning shmuess, which so many talmidim attended. Often on these Friday mornings, when I saw how difficult it was for him to walk up the few steps to my apartment because he suffered from Parkinson's, I told him that he did not have to visit me — instead, I would come to him. However, to no avail — he still kept coming, rain or shine!*
>
> *On these Friday mornings, Rav Nosson Tzvi shared many interesting experiences with me. I think that one of*

2. *Honor Them, Revere Them.*

the ways that a child can show his parents kibbud av va'eim is by sharing with them pleasant experiences that transpired with him throughout the day, as well as his accomplishments — what he achieved from time to time. Parents enjoy hearing good things experienced by their children. I know how much pleasure this gave me.

Today, my younger son Rav Gedaliah, may he continue to be well, who gives a daily shiur in Mirrer Yeshivah, comes to visit me each and every day at around 7 p.m., after he finishes teaching and learning in the yeshivah. In addition, he calls me at least once or twice each day.

What more can a mother ask for?

So anytime your father or mother asks you to do something that you find difficult, tell yourself, "This can't be harder than it was for Rav Nosson Tzvi to trek up a flight of steps every Friday to visit his mother. Every step, every movement, was hard for him. If he could do it, then I can do whatever it is that my parents ask me to do."

A Lesson for Life

"Faiga, I need you to do something for me."

"But, Tatte, I was just about to go visit a friend."

"Tatte" (father) was none other than Rabbi Yisrael Meir HaKohen Kagan, better known as the Chofetz Chaim, which was the first of his many famous *sefarim.* Faiga was his youngest child, who later became Rebbetzin Faiga Zaks, wife of the *gaon* Rabbi Mendel Zaks.

Whenever someone would come to the Chofetz Chaim to buy one of his *sefarim,* the Chofetz Chaim would first have someone check every page of the *sefer* to make sure that there were no missing pages, no blurred pages, no pages glued together, or any other mistakes. If there would be something wrong with the *sefer,* it would be wrong to charge the full price. (In fact, there are

The Chofetz Chaim (pictured with his son R' Aryeh Leib) taught his daughter a lesson that she never forgot.

people who own old copies of the Chofetz Chaim's *sefarim* in which the word מוּגָה [*checked*] was written on the inside cover by the Chofetz Chaim, indicating that the *sefer* was checked and was found free of mistakes.)

One day, someone came to the Chofetz Chaim to purchase three sets of *Mishnah Berurah,* his six-volume work on the laws of daily living. This meant that eighteen volumes needed to be checked. The Chofetz Chaim placed all three sets on the table just as Faiga was putting on her coat to visit her friend. "Faiga, the man needs the *sefarim* today. Please check them."

"But I really want to visit my friend. I'll be happy to check them as soon as I get home!"

"But I need them checked now."

"When I get home, I'll be happy to check thirteen sets! Please let me go now."

The Chofetz Chaim was silent and Faiga took that to mean that she was allowed to leave. So she left.

When she came home, she found thirteen sets of *Mishnah Berurah* on the table.

"But Tatte," she said, "I thought that you needed *three* sets to be checked. Why are there so many on the table?"

"Well," her father replied, "you said that if I would let you go to your friend, you would check thirteen sets when you returned. So here are the thirteen sets."

"But Tatte," Faiga cried, "I didn't really mean that. I just said it because I wanted so badly to go."

"My child," said the Chofetz Chaim, "it's important to learn from an early age that we have to be careful with our words. We have to mean what we say, otherwise we shouldn't say it.

"You said that you would check thirteen sets, so that is what you will have to do."

Years later, Rebbetzin Faiga Zaks told this story and said, "It was a lesson that I never forgot."

Derby to the Rescue

"I can't wait for tonight — wait 'till you see my costume!"

Gershon, a high school-age boy, was very excited. It was the afternoon of Taanis Esther and he was getting ready to join his friends to collect *tzedakah* on Purim night. They had hired a van with a driver to take them around. The boys had decided that rather than wear matching costumes, each boy would choose his own outfit. Gershon's did not cost much. He had found an old pastel shirt, a pair of overalls, and bright suspenders. The clash of colors was just right for Purim!

As he was about to leave the house, Gershon's father handed him an old derby. "How about a hat, Gershon?" he asked with a smile. "It will look great with the rest of your costume!"

Gershon put on the derby and looked in the mirror. He really did not think that the derby added to the costume. In fact, to him it looked a bit strange, and he wondered if the other boys would tease him about it.

But his father seemed so sure that it looked good, and was so happy to add to his costume, that Gershon did not want to disappoint his father.

"Thanks, Dad, the derby looks great," he said with a big smile. "I'm leaving now. Please wish me *hatzlachah*." His father wished him well and Gershon was out the door. He could have removed the derby when he was a safe distance from the house, but decided to keep it on.

The forecast called for snow that evening, and it began to snow only a few minutes after the boys boarded the van. The driver, who was careful and experienced, did his best to navigate the slippery streets. For a while, everything was fine. Because of the weather, the streets were less crowded than usual, and the group visited a few homes in a short amount of time.

The snowfall became heavier and the streets got slippier. As the van turned a corner, it went into a skid and flipped over. Gershon's head went through a window and he lost consciousness. He woke up a short while later and was grateful that he was able to stand up. Aside from a few bruises and some dull pain, he seemed to be fine.

Miraculously, none of the boys had been seriously hurt, but they were taken to the local emergency room, just to make sure. It was there that Gershon finally removed the hat that his father had given him. He was shocked to see that embedded in the derby were pieces of glass from the window that his head had gone through. Had he not been wearing the derby, the glass would most probably have cut into his head.

Pleasing his father had saved Gershon from serious injury.

The Butcher's Reward

R' Yehoshua ben Eilem was a great *talmid chacham* who lived during the time of the Tannaim of the Mishnah. It was revealed to R' Yehoshua in a dream: "Rejoice, for you and Nanas the butcher will be near each other in Gan Eden!"

R' Yehoshua awoke feeling very sad. "I don't understand. From my early youth, I have worked to have *yiras Shamayim* and have put so much effort into my Torah learning. Today, I don't walk four *amos* without wearing *tzitzis* and *tefillin*. I have eighty *talmidim* — and I am only on the level of a butcher?"

R' Yehoshua sent word to his *talmidim* that he would have to find this butcher and speak with him so that he could understand why the two of them would be companions in Gan Eden.

His *talmidim* were determined to help him. They traveled from city to city until they found the place where the butcher lived. When R' Yehoshua entered the city, the local residents sent a message to Nanas: "R' Yehoshua ben Eilem wants to meet you!"

Nanas replied humbly, "Who am I and who were my ancestors that R' Yehoshua is asking about me?"

They told him, "Just come with us."

Nanas thought that they were lying, so he said, "I will not go with you! You're playing games with me!"

They returned to R' Yehoshua and said, "He doesn't want to accompany us!"

R' Yehoshua decided that if Nanas would not come to him, then he would go to Nanas.

When R' Yehoshua arrived at the butcher's home, Nanas fell before his feet and said, "What has happened today that you, who are so great in Torah, have come to visit me?"

R' Yehoshua said, "There is something I must ask you. What is your work and what are you busy with?"

Nanas replied, "My master, I am a butcher. But there is something else that I do. I have an elderly father and mother who are not able to take care of themselves. Every day, I dress them, feed them, and bathe them with my own hands."

R' Yehoshua immediately stood up and kissed Nanas on his head. "My son," he told him, "what you do is so very special! How good, how wonderful! And how fortunate am I that I will merit to be with you in Gan Eden."

From the moment we are born, our parents do everything

for us. Even as we get older and are able to take care of ourselves, our parents continue to guide us, help us, and make sacrifices for us in many ways. When our parents reach old age, the situation is reversed. Then it is the children's turn to take care of their parents. It is not easy to care for elderly parents, but it is a very great mitzvah.

The great Rosh Yeshivah Rabbi Avraham Pam would tell his talmidim that it is good for married children to live in the same city as their parents, because this gives the children many opportunities for kibbud av va'eim.

A Change of Plans

"A *freilichen Purim, Rebbi!"*

It was Purim day in the city of Pressburg; the home of the Rav, Rabbi Shlomo Zalman Unsdorfer, was teeming with visitors. The Rav was very beloved by everyone and his table was crowded with the many *mishloach manos* he and his rebbetzin had received.

The front door opened and in walked Reb Beirish, one of Pressburg's richest Jews, someone who was very close to Rav Unsdorfer. He greeted the Rav, placed a fruit platter and bottle of wine in front of him, and then said in a loud voice for all to hear:

"Aside from the food and drink, there is something else I am adding to the *mishloach manos*!" Reb Beirish withdrew an envelope from his pocket and declared, "In this envelope is a large sum of money that I am giving specifically so that the Rav can finally realize his dream — he can purchase a boat ticket for a trip to Eretz Yisrael!"

"*Mazel tov*!" everyone shouted, and then the crowd erupted in singing and dancing. Everyone knew about Rav Unsdorfer's love of Eretz Yisrael and that he had never been able to make the six-week journey, mainly because of the expense. But with Reb Beirish's gift, the cost was no longer a problem.

After Purim, Rav Unsdorfer began to plan his journey. He booked passage on a ship leaving one week after Pesach. He prepared his assistant to deal with the many problems that come a Rav's way. And of course, he and his rebbetzin spoke often about different situations that could arise while he was away.

Two days after Pesach, Rav Unsdorfer traveled to the city where his parents lived, to say goodbye and to receive their *berachah* for a safe journey.

Finally, the great day arrived. As Rav Unsdorfer placed the final items into his suitcases, a long line of well-wishers was forming outside his home. It seemed that every Jew in Pressburg wanted to offer his good wishes and receive a *berachah* before the Rav departed.

And then it happened. A man on horseback arrived bearing a telegram for the Rav. With trembling hands, Rav Unsdorfer opened the envelope and read the telegram once and then a second time. He was quiet for a minute or so before announcing, "There has been a change in my plans. I will not be going to Eretz Yisrael." He walked over to the wagon driver who had been waiting to take him to the harbor, paid him his fee, and sent him off.

Everyone was stunned. What had happened? What could have made him cancel plans for the journey that had been his dream for so long? His rebbetzin asked the question that was on everyone's mind. Rav Shlomo Zalman answered:

"The telegram that I just received is from my mother. This is what it says:

> *To my dear Shlomo Zalman:*
>
> *As soon as you arrive, please send telegram. I don't want to have to worry more than necessary.*
>
> *Love,*
>
> *Mother"*

Rav Unsdorfer turned to face the crowd outside his home

and said: "Yes, I want so much to visit our holy Eretz Yisrael, the land of our forefathers, the precious land that Hashem has given to His people. But I cannot go if this will mean that my mother, and probably my father too, will be worrying about me for six weeks as I sail the seas. I cannot and will not be the cause of that."

Rav Unsdorfer never visited Eretz Yisrael. And he never regretted his decision.

Advice From a Tzaddik

Before *bachurim* from the Ponovezh Yeshivah returned home for Yom Tov, they would sometimes ask their *mashgiach,* Rabbi Yechezkel (known as Rav Chatzkel) Levenstein: "Rebbi, we know that when we come home for Yom Tov, we will have the opportunity to do the mitzvah of *kibbud av va'eim* throughout the day. Is there anything in particular that we should keep in mind?"

Rav Chatzkel told them, "Yes. It gives a mother great pleasure when her children eat what she serves." Rav Chatzkel was telling

"It gives a mother great pleasure when her children eat what she serves."

his *talmidim* to make sure to eat whatever their mother served for lunch or supper and to make sure to thank her at the end of each meal.

Of course, it's even better to say something like, "Mommy, that was delicious!"

The Rosh Yeshivah of Torah Vodaath, Rabbi Avraham Pam, would describe a scene that is the very opposite of what Rav Chatzkel was suggesting.

> *A bachur comes home from yeshivah and on the table is a tuna salad, with vegetables carefully cut and arranged. He takes one look at the serving plate and says, "Oh, no, tuna* ***again****?"*

We don't have to like everything our mother cooks, but we always have to be careful to show appreciation for her hard work and not hurt her feelings.

A Double Portion of Greatness

Rabbi Moshe Feinstein became a Rav in the Russian town of Uzda when he was a *bachur* of nineteen. One of the local women was assigned the task of cooking his meals. She was proud and grateful to cook for the Rav.

One day, Rav Moshe's sister Chana arrived in Uzda to visit her brother. "I see you are being treated very well," she commented upon seeing him. "You've put on a little bit of weight."

"I *am* being treated well," Rav Moshe replied. "The woman who cooks for me prepares a heaping plate of food for each meal. I always finish whatever she serves; otherwise she might think that I don't like the food. But when she sees my empty plate, she thinks that I'm probably still hungry and she promptly serves me seconds — which I also finish, so as not to hurt her feelings. So, yes — I have put on weight."

Later that day, Chana joined her brother for a meal at the woman's house. She took one bite — and found that it tasted

Rav Moshe, whose middos tovos made him so beloved, would not hurt the woman's feelings.

so awful that she was tempted to spit it out. With a full plate of food staring at her and not wishing to insult her hostess, she saw no way out of her dilemma but to throw the food out the window when the woman was not looking.

In later years, Rav Moshe's sister would relate this story to her grandchildren, expressing her admiration for her brother who ate this woman's cooking day after day for three years, two portions at a time! Difficult as it might have been to eat the poorly prepared food, Rav Moshe found it far more difficult to hurt her feelings.

Dama ben Nesinah

"I need that ring by seven o'clock tonight. If I don't have it by then, the deal is off."

Imagine that you had a ring for sale that was valued at five thousand dollars. Along comes a man who saw a picture of the ring and says, "This looks exactly like the ring that my wife lost when it got washed down the drain. She would love to have it. But I'm flying back to Israel tonight, and I need it by seven p.m. If you can get it to me by then, I'll give you *ten times its value.* Yes, you heard me right — fifty thousand dollars."

You rush home to get the ring, which is in a box under your mattress. You arrive home at six-thirty, dash to your bedroom — and find that your elderly father, whose mind is not what it used to be, is sound asleep on your bed. When his mind was healthy, he surely would have wanted you to wake him up so that you could get the ring. Now, however, he probably would not be happy if he was awakened.

Would you wake him up?

This, says the Gemara (*Kiddushin* 31a), is the *nisayon* (test) that a non-Jew named Dama ben Nesinah faced.

> *It happened that a precious stone was needed for the Ephod worn by the Kohen Gadol. The Chachamim found out that Dama ben Nesinah owned such a stone. They offered him six hundred thousand gold dinars (some say it was eight hundred thousand dinars). But there was a problem: The key to the chest in which the precious stone was kept was under his father's pillow, and Dama did want not to disturb his father, who was asleep. It seems that the Sages went looking elsewhere and found someone else who had the stone they needed.*
>
> *The following year, Hakadosh Baruch Hu rewarded Dama: A parah adumah (red cow) was born in his herd. A parah adumah is very rare and is needed to purify Jews who have come in contact with a dead body. The Sages went to Dama to purchase the cow. Dama said to them: "I know that if I would ask of you all the money in the world you would give it to me. However, I ask of you only that you pay me the amount that I lost last year as a result of not awakening my father."*

The Gemara uses the story of Dama ben Nesinah as an example of outstanding *kibbud av va'eim.* This is difficult to understand. Surely there are also stories of Jews who were willing to sacrifice for *kibbud av va'eim*! Why did the Sages have to use a story of a non-Jew as an example?

Rav Shaul Nathanson answered that the story of Dama ben Nesinah actually shows the greatness of *Klal Yisrael.* Yes, Dama ben Nesinah did something exceptional when he gave up an opportunity to earn a huge profit because he did not want to awaken his father. But what happened the following year? When a *parah adumah* was born in his herd, he told the *Chachamim* that he would "only" charge them the amount he had lost the previous year when they wanted to purchase the *Ephod* stone. In other words, when he had an opportunity to earn the *six hundred thousand* gold *dinars* that he had given up a year earlier, he demanded it as payment.

A Jew would never do such a thing. A Jew would never say, "Last year I lost a lot of money because I did a mitzvah, so now I'm going to demand that amount as payment." A Jew understands that no money in the world can equal the value of a mitzvah. When someone loses money because of a mitzvah, he knows that he really hasn't lost; he has gained something more precious than anything this world has to offer.

That was the attitude of Reb Yaakov, a simple Jew in Kiev, Ukraine...

Not for a Million!

It was the beginning of winter, and Reb Yaakov had a lot on his mind. His little house needed firewood to keep it warm; his children needed boots. And he did not have money for either of those. But he knew that Hashem would help him, as He always did.

Then he saw it: an old, tattered wallet lying on the ground in front of him. He picked it up, opened it, and discovered that it contained no less than seven hundred rubles! Reb Yaakov's first thought was, *Hashem has answered my prayers.*

But then he had a different thought.

This wallet is in such poor condition that its owner could not have been rich. The seven hundred rubles are probably his life's savings, and he was taking the money to make some important purchase. Then he lost his wallet. I can only imagine his pain — I must find him and return the wallet!

A short while later, Reb Yaakov saw a man sobbing as he walked down the street. "*Oy,* what will be... what will be? This *shidduch* is over... it's over! I can't believe this happened. Oy, *Ribbono shel Olam,* how will I tell me wife... my daughter?"

"Reb Yid," Reb Yaakov asked the man kindly, "what happened? Why are you so upset?"

"Why am I so upset?" the man replied. "When you hear my story, you'll understand why. My daughter, my only child, is a *kallah.* My wife and I don't have much money, but for many years, we've been putting away a few rubles at a time to pay for our daughter's wedding and other expenses.

"Before the engagement became official, the *chassan's* parents said that my wife and I had to promise that we would pay for the wedding and also for the new couple's furniture. The money we had saved all these years was just enough to cover these costs. We agreed to the condition and the *mazel tov* was announced.

"This morning, I was on my way to the *chassan's* parents to give them the money we had promised when I tripped and fell. I was bruised and in pain. I was so busy with my injuries that I totally forgot about my wallet; it must have fallen out of my pocket when I fell. When I realized it was missing, I returned to the spot where I fell, but it was nowhere to be seen.

"Most probably some drunkard has found it and is now buying himself some drinks in a bar. *Oy, vey... oy, vey...* such a loss!" And he began to cry once again.

"Reb Yid," said Reb Yaakov, "tell me, how much money was in the wallet?"

"Why are you being so nosy?" the man responded with a

touch of anger. "Does it make a difference now? The money is gone. But if you really want to know, it was seven hundred rubles, not a penny less!"

Hearing the number seven hundred, Reb Yaakov promptly took the wallet out of his pocket, offered it to the man, and said, "Reb Yid, I think this is your wallet."

The man was so shocked he promptly fainted.

When he was revived and somewhat recovered, the man opened his wallet, took out fifty rubles, and offered it to Reb Yaakov as a reward. Reb Yaakov smiled and said, "Thank you, but no thank you. Do you think I would give this mitzvah away for fifty rubles? I wouldn't sell it for a million!"

When the Curtains Opened

Sometimes, when parents get old, they cannot take good care of themselves. It is important that their children and grandchildren make sure that when they go to family weddings, bar mitzvahs, and other places, they look respectable.

We see this in the Torah, when Noach became drunk after the Mabul. When Cham told his brothers that their father was drunk and not properly covered, Shem and Yefes took a blanket and, walking in backwards so that they would not see their father in his disgrace, they covered him. When Noach awoke and found out what had happened, he blessed Shem and Yefes. Chazal tell us that Shem received a greater berachah than Yefes, because he put in greater effort for this mitzvah.

In the following story, we see how the children and grandchildren of Rabbi Avraham Pam were very careful to safeguard his honor at the very end of his long life.

"Do you think he can come to the parlor meeting, Doctor?"

"It's his choice. If Rabbi Pam wants to go, you should let him go. It will be good for him to go."

In the summer of 2001, Rabbi Avraham Pam, the beloved Rosh Yeshivah and leader of *Klal Yisrael,* was very ill. Ten years earlier, when he was seventy-eight years old, Rav Pam, with the help of many others, launched Shuvu, the network of schools in Eretz Yisrael that educates children who otherwise would be in public school.

By the year 2001, when Rav Pam was near the end of his life, Shuvu had taught 10,000 children about the beauty of Torah and mitzvos.

Every summer, a Shuvu parlor meeting is held at a home in Flatbush. People come to hear stories about the students of Shuvu and about the new schools that are opening — and of course, they come to donate money to Shuvu.

As long as Rav Pam was alive, he was the "main attraction" at these meetings. People wanted to receive his *berachah,* and to listen as he spoke words from the heart about the schools and the students whom he cared about so much.

Until his last breath, Rav Pam did everything he could for the children of Shuvu.

But in the summer of 2001, it was not all certain that he would be able to attend the parlor meeting. He had recently come home from the hospital and was very weak. His bedroom was on the second floor of his house, but now it became necessary to install a hospital bed on the ground floor. He needed help with everything, including putting on *tefillin* and getting dressed.

When his family asked his doctor about the parlor meeting, he responded, "If Rabbi Pam wants to go, you should let him go. I have seen that being involved with Shuvu gives him strength. If he goes to the meeting and his being there adds to its success, this will give him strength."

Rav Pam said, "I want to be at the meeting."

The day of the meeting, Rav Pam barely spoke. For a healthy person, speaking does not require much strength, but for someone as sick and weak as Rav Pam, speaking was a strain. And he needed his strength to be able to address the crowd that night.

As the time of the parlor meeting approached, a Hatzolah ambulance pulled up in front of Rav Pam's home. Gently, he was placed on a stretcher and wheeled into the ambulance. His grandson took along Rav Pam's hat and jacket.

When they arrived at the parlor meeting, a large crowd was already there. A partition of curtains was put up so that no one could see Rav Pam as he was being wheeled out of the ambulance. It would not be right for everyone to be watching.

After the stretcher was brought into the house, Rav Pam was very carefully lifted and placed into a comfortable chair behind a desk. Someone put his jacket on him, and then his hat. Only after he was fully dressed and looking dignified were the curtains parted so that everyone could see him.

Rav Pam spoke about Shuvu for five minutes, which was very long considering how weak he was. People were very moved by Rav Pam's *mesiras nefesh* for Shuvu, that he was willing to go through so much difficulty and discomfort to attend the parlor meeting. They said to themselves, "Rav Pam gave Shuvu every ounce of his strength. I have to give more money than I had planned to give."

As Rav Pam had hoped, the meeting was very successful.

And at the same time, his *kavod* had been preserved, as his children and *talmidim* wanted.

Chapter Five
Grandparents

A Lesson From Rav Moshe

Were they excited!

Two brothers, Avraham Yeshayah and Menachem, were going to their grandmother's home for Shabbos. She lived on New York's Lower East Side, not far from where the *gadol hador,* Rabbi Moshe Feinstein, lived. This was toward the end of

Rav Moshe told them: "It would not be right for me to take you away from your grandmother."

Rav Moshe's life, when illness confined him to his apartment. A small *aron kodesh* had been installed in his dining room so that a *minyan* could *daven* there throughout the week. The two boys were excited to be spending Shabbos at their grandmother's for the first time, and also because they planned to *daven* at Rav Moshe's *minyan* that Shabbos.

The plan worked even better than expected. During Shabbos, they had a chance to ask Rav Moshe some questions on the Gemara they were learning in yeshivah. Rav Moshe was so great and at the same time so warm, friendly, and easy to talk to.

After Minchah on Shabbos afternoon, Rav Moshe told his young guests, "The Rebbetzin and I would like to invite you to join us for *shalosh seudos*."

The boys were thrilled. A private *shalosh seudos* with Rav Moshe! It seemed too good to be true.

"Thank you," the older brother said. "I would just like to run over to our grandmother and tell her that we're staying here for *shalosh seudos*."

Rav Moshe looked surprised. "I was not aware that you are visiting your grandmother. How often do you come to her for Shabbos?"

"Well, she comes to us very often, but this is the first time that my brother and I came to her for Shabbos."

"If so," said Rav Moshe, "then it would not be right for me to take you away from your grandmother. You should eat *shalosh seudos* with her."

And that is what they did.

An Original Solution

The man was so happy. He had brought the *gadol hador* a beautiful gift and the *gadol* had accepted it.

The *gadol* was Rabbi Chaim Kanievsky, and the gift was a large silver Chanukah menorah. It is possible that the person

Rav Chaim lights the menorah given to him by his wife's grandfather, Rabbi Aryeh Levin

who had presented the gift had helped Rav Chaim to publish his *sefarim,* or had honored his request to help someone with *tzedakah.* Out of *hakaras hatov,* Rav Chaim felt that it was correct to accept this gift.

But there was a problem. Since his marriage many years before, Rav Chaim had lit a small silver menorah that had been a wedding gift from his wife's grandfather Rabbi Aryeh Levin. He did not want to stop using the menorah that his wife's grandfather had given him. But he knew that the man who had given him the large, new menorah would feel bad if he never used it.

Rav Chaim came up with an original solution. He suggested to his rebbetzin, "I will light the menorah that your grandfather gave us, and you will have in mind to fulfill the mitzvah with my lighting, as you do every year. Later, you will light the new menorah, but without a *berachah,* since you have already fulfilled the mitzvah."

Rebbetzin Kanievsky liked this idea very much. For the rest of her life, she lit the other menorah. Because she was a famous *tzaddekes* to whom many women felt close, there were always women present when she lit the menorah. It was a true *pirsumei nisa,* publicizing the Chanukah miracle. The man who had presented Rav Chaim with the menorah was probably very happy knowing that his menorah was used in such a special way. Rav Chaim and his rebbetzin were very happy that they were able to continue using the menorah that had been given to them by their grandfather, one of the most beloved *gedolim* of recent times.

Chapter Six
Learning From Our Gedolim

Like a Guest in His Own Home

"Father, is it all right if I use this *sefer*?"

The speaker was the legendary Kaminetz Rosh Yeshivah, Rabbi Boruch Ber Leibowitz. It was in the middle of World War I. Rav Boruch Ber's father, Rav Shmuel Dovid, had

Anyone who did not know the truth would have thought that Rav Boruch Ber had moved in with his parents.

been a wealthy man, but the war caused his business to collapse and now he was poor. He and his wife had moved in with their son and his family.

Anyone who did not know the truth would have thought that Rav Boruch Ber had moved in with his parents. Anytime he wanted to use something, he would ask his parents' permission. He did this not only to honor them, but so that they should not feel like poor people.

He did not wait for them to ask him to get them something or do something for them. Every so often he would approach his father and mother and ask, "Can I get you something? Are you sure that you have everything you need?"

One of the *gedolim* who had a close-up view of Rav Boruch Ber's *kibbud av va'eim* said, "He is so busy with his parents — I am amazed that he has time to learn!"

Rav Shmuel Dovid regularly attended his son's *shiurim.* Before beginning each *shiur,* Rav Boruch Ber would approach his father for permission, and at the conclusion of the *shiur,* he would ask, "My dear father, did I say a good *shiur* today?"

Once, a soldier approached Rav Shmuel Dovid and said, "Give me your watch!" But Rav Shmuel Dovid did not want to part with one of the few possessions he still owned. Suddenly, the soldier withdrew a dagger and was about to stab Rav Shmuel Dovid. Rav Boruch Ber did not waste a second. He lunged at the soldier and screamed, "Do it to me, not to him!"

Suddenly, an army officer appeared. "What's going on here?" he shouted. Gazing at the soldier in obvious anger, he said, "Get out of here and don't ever touch these people again."

Who was that officer? No one will ever know. Rav Boruch Ber later said, "The *zechus* of the mitzvah of *kibbud av* is what saved me."

The day came when remaining in their city became too dangerous; it was time to flee to Vilna. Traveling was very difficult for the elderly Rav Shmuel Dovid, but Rav Boruch Ber did his best to make it as easy as possible. When they came to a fence that had to be scaled, Rav Boruch Ber lay down on the ground so that his father could stand on him, making it easier to climb over the fence.

Rav Shmuel Dovid took ill in Vilna and passed away. For a long time, Rav Boruch Ber worried that perhaps he didn't do enough to try to save his father's life. Then he met the Chofetz Chaim, who was able to calm his fears. Rav Boruch Ber would later say, "The Chofetz Chaim gave me new life!"

He named his famous *sefer* on Gemara *Bircas Shmuel* in memory of his father. Rav Boruch Ber planned to also write a *sefer* on Chumash in memory of his mother, but passed away before he was able to do so.

Toward the end of her life, Rav Boruch Ber's mother-in-law, Rebbetzin Zimmerman, moved in with him and his family. When he would hear her calling, he would run and say, "I'm coming, I'm coming..." so that she would know that help was on the way.

On Shabbos, Rav Boruch Ber would sit at one end of the table and his mother-in-law would sit at the opposite end. One Shabbos, some *talmidim* came to visit their rebbi, and a lively discussion took place. Rebbetzin Zimmerman said to her granddaughter, "If I could, I would move closer so that I could hear what they are saying!" Rav Boruch Ber heard his mother-in-law's comment and immediately moved his chair closer to hers.

So That His Mother Could Hear

"Shlomo Zalman, do you think I can use it on Shabbos?"

"I'm not sure, Mama, but I'm going to do my very best to answer your question."

It was the early 1930s in the holy city of Yerushalayim. Rebbetzin Tziviah Auerbach had become hard of hearing and had just received her first pair of hearing aids. Hearing aids, which run on batteries, had recently been invented, and Rebbetzin Auerbach wanted to know if they could be used on Shabbos. She never missed being in shul on Shabbos morning, but without her hearing aids, she would not be able to hear the *chazzan* or *baal korei.*

As a relatively new invention, hearing aids were quite expensive. Rebbetzin Auerbach did not have an extra penny to spare; she and her husband, Rav Chaim Leib, could barely provide their children with the most basic foods. From where did they get the money to buy hearing aids?

Their son Shlomo Zalman was an outstanding student at Yeshivas Eitz Chaim in Yerushalayim. When a boy scored well on a written or oral test, he would be rewarded with a few coins and a gift certificate to purchase *sefarim*. One day, Shlomo Zalman approached the *menahel* and asked, "Would it be possible if from now on I could receive money instead of a gift certificate?"

Knowing Shlomo Zalman, the *menahel* was surprised. "Is there anything that you would like to buy more than *sefarim*?"

As a boy, Rav Shlomo Zalman saved up his money to buy his mother hearing aids.

"Well, my mother has become hard of hearing; she is almost completely deaf. She mentioned that if she had something called a 'hearing aid' she would be able to hear much better. I would like to save up money until I have enough so that I can buy my mother a hearing aid."

And that is how Rebbetzin Auerbach got her hearing aids. But she never used them on Shabbos because none of the *poskim* in Eretz Yisrael at that time understood exactly how batteries or electricity work, so they could not decide whether hearing aids could be used on Shabbos. And there was no *sefer* that discussed this new question.

By the time Rav Shlomo Zalman was a young man in his twenties, he was already known as an outstanding *talmid chacham* who had great knowledge of halachah. The day would come when Rav Shlomo Zalman Auerbach would be one of the world's greatest *poskim.*

In order to help his mother, Rav Shlomo Zalman spent many months learning everything that had to do with the topic of electricity and its use on Shabbos. The result was his first *sefer,* called *Me'orei HaEish,* all about electricity. When this *sefer* reached Vilna in faraway Lithuania and was read by the *posek hador* Rabbi Chaim Ozer Grodzensky, he declared with excitement: **אוֹר חָדָשׁ עַל צִיּוֹן תָּאִיר** (*A great light will shine upon Tzion [Yerushalayim]*), because he could tell that the young author of this *sefer* would one day become one of *Klal Yisrael's* great *poskim* and leaders.

Perhaps his ability to write such an amazing *sefer* at such a young age had to do with the fact that the reason he wrote it was to help his mother.

For the Sake of His Mother-in-law

Until the end of his life, Rav Shlomo Zalman lived in the home that had belonged to his father-in-law, Rabbi Leib Ruchamkin. He showed his parents-in-law unusual honor. Even after his father-in-law passed away, Rav Shlomo Zalman refused to sit at the head of the table, out of respect for his mother-in-law who was still living. He may have been a world-famous Torah leader, but in his house, he considered himself just a son-in-law who had a mitzvah to honor his mother-in-law.

It is also a mitzvah for a husband to honor his wife. When distributing the portions of challah at the Shabbos and Yom Tov meals, Rav Shlomo Zalman made a point of giving his wife and his mother-in-law their portions at the same time.

His mother-in-law lived to age ninety-eight. In her last years, she needed almost constant care. Some well-meaning people told Rav Shlomo Zalman, "You and your wife are not so young yourselves. Why not place your mother-in-law in a nursing home?" Rav Shlomo Zalman rejected these suggestions. True, it was not easy, but he and his rebbetzin felt that as long as they could take care of Rebbetzin Ruchamkin, they should do it. It is possible that his mother-in-law lived so long because of the loving care she received at home.

During those last years when she could no longer attend family *simchahs,* Rav Shlomo Zalman made sure to always bring home a piece of cake for his mother-in-law and tell her with a smile, "This cake is from the *bris* of..."

In his *tzavaah* (will) Rav Shlomo Zalman wrote, "My tombstone should be of standard size, and certainly no higher than those of my parents ע״ה."

During the *shivah* for Rav Shlomo Zalman, a non-religious taxi driver told a passenger that he had heard about Rav Shlomo Zalman's instructions regarding his tombstone. He commented with a sigh, "My children hardly look at me, and the Rav was concerned about the honor of his parents who died many years ago. Ah, if I would be a bit younger, I would become a *baal teshuvah...*"

A Tale of Two Chairs

"Wow! That's a beautiful chair. It's for the Rosh Yeshivah, right?"

"Actually, it's for his father."

Rabbi Shlomo Zalman Auerbach's oldest son Rav Shmuel was recognized as a *gadol* in his father's lifetime. Rav Shlomo Zalman lived near his son's yeshivah in Yerushalayim's Shaarei Chesed neighborhood. In his later years, Rav Shlomo Zalman would *daven* Shacharis in his son's yeshivah. Of course, his son prepared a seat for him near his own seat at the eastern wall alongside the *aron kodesh.*

Rav Shmuel sat on a regular chair, and so did his father. All the chairs in the beis midrash were basically the same. As Rav Shlomo Zalman aged and grew more frail, someone had an idea. "Why don't we buy a comfortable armchair for the Rosh Yeshivah's father? After all, Shacharis lasts about an hour, and at his age, it's probably hard to sit in a regular chair for so long."

Rav Shmuel thought it was an excellent idea, and one day,

Rav Shmuel would not sit on the chair as long as his father was alive.

members of the *minyan* proudly brought into the beis midrash a beautiful cushioned armchair. They placed it at the spot where Rav Shlomo Zalman *davened* every morning.

The next morning, those who had arrived early for Shacharis watched as Rav Shlomo Zalman entered the beis midrash. They were expecting his face to light up with his trademark smile when he saw the new chair.

They were very disappointed.

Rav Shlomo Zalman seemed to be upset.

"Is something wrong?" someone finally asked him.

"Thank you so much for the chair," Rav Shlomo Zalman said. "It's very beautiful and I'm sure it's very comfortable. It was very thoughtful of you to buy it for me. But I can't sit in it. You see, I'm not the Rosh Yeshivah. Rav Shmuel is the Rosh Yeshivah. It would not be right for me to sit in an elegant chair while the Rosh Yeshivah sits in a plain chair."

The next morning, there were two identical, elegant armchairs side by side, one for Rav Shlomo Zalman and one for his son. Rav Shlomo Zalman was pleased.

But Rav Shmuel was not. He could not bring himself to sit in the chair.

"You see," he explained to his *talmidim*, "there are only two such chairs in the entire beis midrash. If I were to sit on such a chair next to my father, it would give the impression that I consider myself equal to my father. This would be disrespectful."

Rav Shmuel continued to sit on a plain chair. Only after his father passed away did Rav Shmuel begin to use the armchair.

Give Them Nachas

"Rabbi, are you sure that's where they should be delivered?"

"Yes, I'm sure. And I'll be there waiting when the truck arrives."

Rabbi Shimshon Pincus, who served as Rav of Ofakim in southern Israel, had just completed a *sefer* that was to become famous in the Torah world. *She'arim BiTefillah,* which teaches all about *davening,* is such an outstanding *sefer* that it is hard to believe that it was written by someone who lived in our times.

When the printer called him to say that the first boxes of *sefarim* were ready for delivery, Rav Shimshon said that he didn't want them delivered to his house, or to a company that distributes *sefarim*. Instead, he wanted them delivered to the home of his parents, Rabbi and Mrs. Avrohom Chaim Pincus, who lived in Yerushalayim. He knew that his parents would have tremendous pleasure from seeing the *sefer* that their son had written, and he wanted them to enjoy that *nachas* as soon as possible.

His parents lived in an apartment building, and the printer's truck driver would bring the boxes of *sefarim* to the ground floor. It would be Rav Shimshon's task to bring them from the ground floor to his parents' apartment.

When a *talmid* heard about this, he said to Rav Shimshon,

"Thank you so much, but I prefer to do the mitzvah myself."

"Rebbi does not have to go to meet the truck. I will be happy to wait in front of the building for the delivery and then carry the boxes upstairs to Rebbi's parents."

Rav Shimshon was touched. "Thank you so much for offering, but I prefer to do this mitzvah myself. It wouldn't be the same if someone else opened the first box and presented my father and mother with the very first copy of *She'arim BiTefillah*. And carrying the boxes upstairs is part of the mitzvah. I really don't want anyone to do it for me."

> *We don't have to write sefarim to give our parents nachas. There are so many ways to make them proud of us. We should not be modest when it comes to giving our parents nachas — meaning, we should not hide our accomplishments from our parents. They deserve to take pride in what we have achieved.*

This lesson was once taught in Camp Agudah by none other than the Rosh Yeshivah of the Philadelphia yeshivah, Rabbi Shmuel Kamenetsky.

Rav Shmuel was a special guest at the camp that Shabbos. On Motza'ei Shabbos, Rabbi Dovid Frischman approached Rav

Rav Shmuel taught that we should not pass up an opportunity to give our parents nachas.

Shmuel. "Tonight at the Masmidim program's *melaveh malkah,* I will be giving a special Gemara *shiur*. I would like to invite the Rosh Yeshivah to attend." Rav Shmuel said that he would be very happy to attend the *melaveh malkah* and be present for the *shiur.*

That night, as Rabbi Frischman ended his *shiur* and sat down, he noticed Rav Shmuel coming toward him. Rabbi Frischman thought, "It looks like the Rosh Yeshivah wants to ask me a question about something I said in the *shiur.*"

He was wrong. Rav Shmuel *did* want to speak to him about the *shiur,* but not about what he had said in the *shiur.*

As Rav Shmuel got closer, Rabbi Frischman noticed that Rav Shmuel looked upset.

"Reb Dovid," the Rosh Yeshivah said, "I don't understand. Your father is here in camp. How could you not invite your father to the *melaveh malkah* so that he could listen to your *shiur* and have *nachas*?"

Rav Dovid's father, Reb Meir Frischman, was the longtime director of Camp Agudah. Because he was so busy running the camp, it was very rare that he attended a camp *melaveh malkah.* That is why his son had not thought to invite him. But upon hearing what Rav Shmuel said, Rabbi Dovid Frischman realized that Rav Shmuel was right. His father would have derived great pleasure from hearing his son's special *shiur,* and he should have invited him.

Rabbi Dovid Frischman has told this story in public so that others can learn from his mistake.

A Question and an Answer

"May I ask a question? What did the Rav do that he became so great?"

A ten-year-old boy asked that question to none other than Rabbi Avraham Yeshayah Karelitz, the famous author of *Sefer Chazon Ish*. It happened when the Chazon Ish, as he was known, came to the local yeshivah in Kfar Saba to test the *talmidim*. The Chazon Ish was the leader of the generation and one of its greatest *poskim*. The boy asked the question sincerely; he really wanted to know how someone becomes a *gadol hador*.

The Chazon Ish was very humble and was not comfortable speaking about himself. But the question was an important one, and he felt that he had to give the boy an answer.

After a few moments of silence, the Chazon Ish told the boy, "I was always very careful with *kibbud av va'eim*. And I tried very hard never to cause my parents to worry or become upset."

The Steipler Gaon, Rabbi Yaakov Yisrael Kanievsky, was married to the Chazon Ish's sister. The Bnei Brak apartments of the Steipler and the Chazon Ish were in the same building and in fact shared a wall. Rabbi Chaim Kanievsky became very close to his uncle the Chazon Ish. In later years, Rav Chaim would speak about his uncle's *kibbud eim*. (The Chazon Ish's father had passed away many years earlier.)

The Chazon Ish used every available minute to study Torah. Even so, he spent a half-hour every day visiting his mother and discussing anything she wanted to talk about. One day the

The Chazon Ish said: "I was always very careful with kibbud av va'eim."

Chazon Ish did not feel well, and therefore did not walk the few blocks to visit his mother. The next morning, Rav Chaim, who was a child at the time, heard her say, "I wonder why Avraham Yeshayah didn't come yesterday." Chaim went home and repeated these words to his uncle. Immediately, the Chazon Ish grabbed his hat and jacket and started running to his mother's apartment.

Rav Chaim recalled, "I could not catch up with him, no matter how hard I tried. He ran because of *kibbud av va'eim,* because his mother was worried."

There was a small shul in the Chazon Ish's apartment that had *minyanim* throughout the week. Some mornings, the Chazon Ish's mother would *daven* in the small women's section. As soon as the Chazon Ish caught sight of her, he would grab a *shtender* and begin dragging it toward her so that she could put her *siddur* on it. This was not easy for him because, for much of his life, the Chazon Ish was in poor health. Sometimes, when his rebbetzin would see him dragging the *shtender,* she would hurry over, take it from him, and drag it to where her mother-in-law was sitting.

The Chazon Ish would learn until he had no strength left. Sometimes, when he finally closed his *sefer,* he did not have the strength to walk to his bed, so he would lie down on the floor near his table.

On one such day, as he lay there on the floor, there was a light tapping on the door. The Chazon Ish jumped up from the floor as if bitten by a snake and hurried to open the door. His mother had come to visit, and he busied himself with taking care of her.

A *talmid* who was present asked him, "How did the Rav know that it was his mother at the door?"

"I recognized her knock," the Chazon Ish replied.

"But from where did the Rav draw the strength to jump up and hurry to take care of her?" the *talmid* persisted. "Only moments ago, the Rav had no strength!"

The Chazon Ish smiled. "For a mother, a person always has strength."

A Reason to Delay

"Mazel tov — it's a boy!"

There was great joy in the Badani* home. A healthy baby is always reason for much joy and thanks to Hashem. And when a boy is born, plans have to begin almost immediately for the *bris milah,* which hopefully will be on time on the eighth day of the baby's life.

When Mrs. Badani came home from the hospital with the baby, the *mohel* came to the house. After examining the baby, he told the parents that he saw no reason why the *bris* could not be on time. The Badanis were overjoyed.

"So what time is *davening* going to be?" the *mohel* asked, so that he could put the *bris* into his schedule. "I assume that the *bris* will take place as soon as Shacharis is over."

The Torah tells us that Avraham Avinu arose early in the morning when he took Yitzchak to the *Akeidah*. From there, we learn that *zerizim makdimim l'mitzvos* — those who are very eager to do mitzvos do them at the earliest possible time. That is why a *bris* is usually held right after Shacharis.

However, this time Mr. Badani was not sure.

"My father plans to fly in from New York for the *bris* that morning," he explained, "and I have to find out what time his flight is due to land in Tel Aviv, and what time his taxi is due to arrive in Yerushalayim. Then we can schedule the *bris."*

Later that day, Mr. Badani spoke with his father. His plane was due to land at seven a.m. and he planned to *daven* Shacharis on the plane. If the plane landed on schedule, he would probably be in a taxi by eight o'clock and would be in Yerushalayim, taking into account regular morning traffic, by nine o'clock. They could schedule the *bris* for nine-thirty.

This was assuming that the plane would land on time, that there would be no delays getting off the plane, getting the luggage, and going through passport control. And it also assumed that the traffic that morning would be normal, not unusually heavy.

Even if everything worked out, Mr. Badani's father would probably be tense until he arrived at the shul where the *bris* would be held. After all, he would be making a tiring and expensive trip just to be at the *bris*. He would be checking his watch the whole time and praying, "Please, Hashem, help me to get there on time!"

Mr. Badani said to his wife, "I'm not sure what we should do. The rule that *zerizim makdimim l'mitzvos* means we should make the *bris* as early as possible. But is it right to do that if it will make my father tense?"

Mr. and Mrs. Badani agreed that they should present their dilemma to a *talmid chacham*. Mr. Badani brought the question to Rabbi Shlomo Zalman Auerbach, and his answer left no room for doubt.

"There is no question that *kibbud av va'eim* is more important than the teaching of *zerizim makdimim l'mitzvos*. It is important that your father come to the *bris* relaxed, not tense and worried that he might not make it in time.

"It is important that your father come to the bris relaxed."

"Make the *bris* at around 11:30. That way, it will still be in the morning, before midday, but late enough that your father will have plenty of time to get there and maybe even have a short nap beforehand."

A rebbi in a Lakewood yeshivah was making a *bris* for his son. He wanted to schedule Shacharis for a very early hour so that by the time the *seudah* ended, he would still have enough time to get to his classroom on time. He called his rebbi, Rabbi Elya Svei (who, together with יבל״ח Rabbi Shmuel Kamenetsky, served as Rosh Yeshivah of the Philadephia yeshivah), to make sure that this was a good idea.

Rav Svei liked the idea very much — except for one thing. "Both your parents and your in-laws live in Brooklyn. If *davening* is so early, they will have to get up at about 4 a.m. to be there on time. It's not right to make your parents and in-laws get up so early."

"But, Rebbi," the baby's father replied, "my parents and in-laws are both coming to Lakewood the night before the *bris*. They will not have to get up so early."

"In that case," said Rav Svei, "your plan is a very good one."

"It's not right to make your parents and in-laws get up so early."

Advice From Rav Moshe

As a child, Rabbi Reuven Feinstein had no idea that his father Rav Moshe was a leader of his generation. That's because at home, Rav Moshe seemed quite ordinary.

But his love for his children was very obvious. Even when the Shabbos table had important guests, Rav Moshe sat his son Reuven, the youngest in the family, right next to him. On cold winter mornings, Rav Moshe would put his children's clothing on the radiators so that when the children woke up and got dressed, their clothing would be warm.

In Rav Reuven's words, "As a child, I always looked at my father as a regular person. I thought that this is how all fathers were. I played marbles next to his desk, and that was perfectly fine with him."

When Rav Moshe was dealing with the question of whether or not a refrigerator may be opened on Shabbos when its compressor is off, he invited his young son to lie down on the floor next to him and examine the motor of the refrigerator.

When did Rav Reuven realize that his father was a world-famous *posek*? As a teenager, he became a *talmid* of the Telshe Yeshivah in Cleveland. It happened very often that rebbeim

As a child, Rav Reuven was always seated next to his father at the table.

asked him, “Reuven, next time you speak to your father, could you ask him what the halachah is if someone...” Seeing how these *talmidei chachamim* valued his father’s opinion so much made Rav Reuven realize that his father was very great.

When we speak to a Rav or Rosh Yeshivah, we don’t say, “Last week, you said...” Instead, we say, “Last week, the Rav said...” or, “Last week, the Rosh Yeshivah said...

But when we speak to our parents, we don’t say to our mother, “Mommy said,” or to our father, “Daddy said.” We say, “You said.” The Chasam Sofer explains that because of the special closeness between a parent and child, it is correct to speak to a parent this way.

The more Rav Reuven realized how great his father was, the more he wanted to address him in “third person,” to say, “The Tatte said” instead of “You said.” When he asked his father permission to address him this way, Rav Moshe was not happy about it. “It is not necessary,” he replied, “but I see that you mean it sincerely, so I will allow it.”

When Rav Reuven turned twenty, he wrote a letter to his father, asking for advice that would help him throughout his life. Rav Moshe felt that his letter back to his son was so important that he published it in his famous *sefer Igros (Letters of) Moshe.*

In that letter, Rav Moshe wrote about the importance of *limud haTorah* and of making sure to avoid becoming angry or arrogant. And then he wrote that Rav Reuven should be very careful to honor his mother. Rav Moshe explained that at times it can be very hard to show proper *kibbud av va'eim* because we are so familiar with and feel so close to our parents. Therefore, we might sometimes forget that we must *always* act toward them and speak to them with proper respect.

This point reminded me of a story. A man was once asked to drive Rav Moshe from the Catskill Mountains to the Lower East Side where Rav Moshe lived. The man was not told who

Rav Moshe's advice to his son applies to all of us.

his passenger was and had never met Rav Moshe. This was in the days before *gedolim* photos were common, so the man had no idea that the passenger sitting next to him was a *gadol hador*.

Rav Moshe carried on a very friendly conversation with the driver and the driver felt very comfortable with his passenger, who said that he was "a rebbi in a yeshivah." (Actually, Rav Moshe was the Rosh HaYeshivah of his yeshivah and also the leading *posek* of his time.) The driver spoke to Rav Moshe as he would speak to a friend.

A few days later, when the driver found out that his passenger was the famous Rav Moshe Feinstein, he began to worry that perhaps he had not spoken to Rav Moshe with the proper respect. He told someone, "For a few nights, I had trouble sleeping. Perhaps I said something, a joke or some comment, that should not be said to a *gadol hador*?"

We are with our parents day after day from birth, so we become very comfortable in front of them. Because we are so close to them it's possible that we could sometimes say a comment or a joke, or act in a certain way, that is not proper *kibbud av va'eim*.

Rav Moshe's advice to his son applies to all of us: Let's try our best to always speak and act toward our parents with proper respect.

The Wooden Spoon

"Father, what are you making?" the little boy asked.

"Oh, this is a wooden spoon for Grandpa. You see, Grandpa is very old and his hands shake. When he eats at our table with regular silverware, the metal bangs against his plate and makes a lot of noise. This wooden spoon will be much quieter."

The little boy seemed troubled. "But Father, is Grandpa going to feel bad to be the only one at the table using a wooden spoon?"

"Well," his father replied, "we can't worry about that. Mother and I don't enjoy eating our meals with all that noise from his silverware. He'll just have to get used to it."

The next day, the father came into his son's room and found him busy at work, trying to shape a piece of thin wood into some sort of item.

"Son, what are you doing?" the father asked.

"Oh," the boy said quietly, "I'm trying to make a wooden spoon to give you when you will be an old man."

Rabbi Manis Mandel would tell this *mashal* to his students when speaking about *kibbud av va'eim*. He would say, "Children, the way you act toward your parents is the way that your children will act toward you. Make sure that you treat your parents with proper respect."

Rabbi Chaim Kanievsky said that we often see how true this is. Rav Chaim even found a hint to this in the Torah.

When Eisav brought food to his father Yitzchak, the Torah says וַיָּבֵא לְאָבִיו, *And he brought (the food) to his father (Bereishis*

"Children, the way you act toward your parents is the way that your children will act toward you."

27:31). When these two words are read backward, they also spell וַיָּבֵא לְאָבִיו! This teaches that a child "gets back" what he gives to his parents. The way a child treats his parents is the way that his children will treat him.

Who Goes First?

Dear reader: I would like to share with you a mistake that I once made. I hope that you will learn from my mistake, and this will be a *zechus* for both of us.

For many years, my elderly parents-in-law would come to spend Yom Tov with us. Walking was difficult for my father-in-law, so we would *daven* at the *minyan* closest to my house, at Yeshivah Zichron Meilech in Brooklyn. In those years, the yeshivah was led by one of the *gedolei hador*, Rabbi Chaim Leib Epstein.

After *davening* every Yom Tov morning, the members of the *minyan* would file past the Rosh Yeshivah to wish him a *gut Yom Tov.* One morning as I filed past Rav Chaim Leib, it seemed to me that he had an unhappy look on his face. I had seen that look once before. Someone in the *minyan* was doing something that wasn't terrible, but the Rosh Yeshivah disapproved of it. He did

Rav Chaim Leib taught me a lesson for life.

not want to give the person *mussar* and criticize him directly, so he just looked upset. The Rosh Yeshivah was probably hoping that either the person would figure out the reason for his unhappiness, or someone else would figure it out and tell the person to stop what he was doing. (The person himself figured it out and stopped what he had been doing.)

So, now, I said to myself, *Why does the Rosh Yeshivah look upset? Could it be that I'm doing something wrong?*

And then it hit me. I was walking in front of my father-in-law as we filed past the Rosh Yeshivah. That was not respectful. I should have taken care to see that he walked in front of me.

I made sure never to make that mistake again.

A Strange Discovery

"What is this doing here?"

"I don't know. Maybe Mama put it here by mistake. Let's ask her."

After the tzaddik Rabbi Shmuel Aharon Yudelevitch passed away, his sons were looking through the many pages of handwritten *divrei Torah* he had left behind. And between all the papers, they discovered a recipe for apple strudel!

When they asked their mother, Rebbetzin Rasha, if she knew anything about it, she smiled and explained:

"As you know, Tatte would travel up north a few times a year to visit his mother, who lived in Kfar Tavor from the time she remarried after Tatte's father passed away. On one of his visits, he came into the house and she said, 'Shmuel Aharon, you came at just the right time! I have a delicious apple strudel about to come out of the oven. Sit down and I'll cut you a slice.'

"Now, children," Rav Shmuel Aharon's rebbetzin continued, "you and I know that food was really not important to your father. It made no difference to him what he was served — it was all the same to him. Of course, he always thanked me for everything I made, but I knew that he hardly realized what he was eating.

"He wanted to make his mother feel good, so with each bite of the strudel, he told her how delicious it was. At one point he said, 'Ah, it would be good if Rasha would have this recipe!'

"'That's a wonderful idea,' his mother replied. 'Here's a piece of paper and a pen. I'll tell you the recipe and you can write it down.'

"And so," Rebbetzin Rasha concluded, "that's how the recipe for apple strudel came to be found among your father's papers. He told me about it when he returned from his visit, but we both forgot about it after that. As I said, food was really not important to him. And the paper remained in his drawer until you found it today."

The Greatest Blessing

It is not a coincidence, said Rabbi Aharon Leib Shteinman, that *gedolei Yisrael* excel in *kibbud av va'eim*. As examples, he said that Rabbi Chaim Soloveitchik showed exceptional honor for his father, the Beis HaLevi; and the Chazon Ish excelled in the respect that he showed his parents.

Rabbi Chaim Soloveitchik's kibbud av va'eim was exceptional.

The Mishnah (*Kiddushin* 1:10) says that someone who is careful to do a particular mitzvah will earn great blessing in this world. Rabbi Chaim Kanievsky would say that according to *Talmud Yerushalmi,* this mishnah is speaking about *kibbud av va'eim.* It is no wonder, then, that those who excelled in *kibbud av va'eim* and studied with great effort became great in Torah — what greater blessing can there be?

The way Rav Chaim honored his parents in their lifetime is an example for all of us to follow. In the last years of his mother's life, he would visit her every day. After his mother passed away, Rav Chaim's widowed sister Rebbetzin Barzam moved in with her father and took care of all his needs. Rav Chaim thought that his father probably did not want him to visit every day, so he began to visit every few days.

One day, the Steipler remarked, "A father also enjoys when his son visits him." Rav Chaim understood that his father would like him to visit every day just as he had done when his mother was alive. He resumed his daily visits and continued to do so until his father passed away on 23 Menachem Av 5745 (1985).

Many *sefarim* have been published that contain the *piskei halachah* (halachic rulings) of Rav Chaim. Until the Steipler passed away in 5745 (1985), Rav Chaim would not rule on halachic questions because he felt it was not respectful to do so as long as his father was alive and could answer such questions.

There was one exception. A very nervous woman was always worried that she might be doing something that was against halachah. The Steipler instructed Rav Chaim to always answer her questions because he knew that her constant worry and nervousness was affecting her health.

Once, when the Steipler was preparing the introduction for one of his famous *sefarim,* he wanted to quote a teaching of *Chazal,* "Pity on the person who is thought to learn well and be a tzaddik, but is really neither." The Steipler was truly humble and it bothered him that people considered him a great *talmid chacham* and a tzaddik (even though he was both).

But in order to publish this teaching, the Steipler needed to know its source. Was it a Midrash, and if so, where was it located? He wasn't sure, so he asked his son, who seemed to know the source for everything. Strangely, this time Rav Chaim said that he did not know the source of the teaching.

As long as his father, the Steipler Gaon, was alive, Rav Chaim (walking behind him) would not rule on halachic questions.

Years later, after his father had passed away, Rav Chaim told his grandchildren, "I knew the source of that teaching, but I felt that it would not be respectful to tell it to my father, since he wanted to write it about himself!"

Once, a young woman asked Rebbetzin Kanievsky to request a *berachah* from Rav Chaim for her sake. She was a publisher of Hebrew books and had misplaced a computer hard drive that contained a book she had been given to publish. If she could not find the hard drive, she would lose a lot of money.

Rav Chaim told his rebbetzin that he could not give this woman the *berachah* she was seeking. This woman's father was a *talmid chacham* who had written a number of *sefarim*. When this woman was younger, she had carelessly caused some of her father's writings to become lost, and they were never recovered. Apparently, Rav Chaim felt that what was happening to her now was a punishment for the loss she had caused her father.

When the Rebbetzin told the woman what Rav Chaim had said, she immediately went to her father to ask *mechilah* for what she had done. He told her that he forgave her wholeheartedly. When the Rebbetzin told this to Rav Chaim, he gave his *berachah* that the woman find what she was missing. She found it the next morning.

His Mission in This World

Rabbi Pinchos Dovid HaLevi Horowitz, the first Bostoner Rebbe, never wanted to come to America — but Hashem decreed that he should. On a trip from Yerushalayim to Europe, Rav Pinchos Dovid was suddenly stranded when World War I broke out. He had to flee for his life, but could not get back to Eretz Yisrael. The only available ship was sailing to America. And that is how he ended up becoming a Rebbe in Boston, Massachusetts.

He had two sons and a daughter. After he passed away at a

Rav Levi Yitzchok (left) felt that his mission in this world was to make his father's coming to Boston worthwhile.

fairly young age in 1941 in New York, where he had moved a few years earlier, his married son Rav Moshe became the Bostoner Rebbe of New York. His younger son, Rav Levi Yitzchok, married Rebbetzin Raichel a year later. Rav Levi Yitzchok did not want to be a Rebbe. Being very modest and even a bit shy, he thought that he would live in New York and be a businessman who, of course, would set aside time every day to learn Torah.

But Hashem had other plans for him. Rav Levi Yitzchok tried polishing diamonds... and saw that he was not good at it. He invested some money in a stationery business... and the business failed.

Meanwhile, the small group of Bostoner chassidim back in Boston were calling almost every week. "Please, Rav Levi Yitzchok — our shul has no leader. We need a leader. Please, come and be our Rebbe just as your father was for so many years."

Rav Levi Yitzchok did not want to be a Rebbe. But he knew that it had been his father's desire for his older brother, Rav Moshe, to be Bostoner Rebbe in his shul in New York, and for

Rav Levi Yitzchok to be Bostoner Rebbe in his shul in Boston. If he became Rebbe, he would be carrying on his father's holy mission to bring the light of Torah and *chassidus* to the people of Boston.

He accepted the position and became the Bostoner Rebbe of Boston in 1944. By the time he passed away in 2009, Rav Levi Yitzchok had brought thousands closer to Hashem, had established a second *kehillah* and shul in Har Nof, Yerushalayim, in addition to the one in Boston, and was recognized as one of the great Torah leaders of his generation.

All his life, he was careful to fulfill every *minhag* of his father. And he would say, "My mission in this world is to make my father's coming to Boston worthwhile."

He certainly accomplished that.

Chapter Seven
Honor Forever

Kitzur Shulchan Aruch states that a person can do the mitzvah of kibbud av va'eim even after his parents have left this world. Every mitzvah that the child does, every word of davening and learning, every act of chesed, is a zechus for his parents and brings them great pleasure in Gan Eden.

"Just Keep Doing Such Mitzvos"

Rabbi Tzvi Kowalsky grew up in Bnei Brak, where he became close to Rabbi Avraham Yeshayah Karelitz, the famed Chazon Ish. One year before Yom Tov, as young Tzvi was about to return home from yeshivah after being away for many months, the Chazon Ish told him, "Before leaving for home, review the halachos of *kibbud av va'eim.*" The Chazon Ish knew that Tzvi would have honored his parents in any case, but he wanted to make sure that he would do it in the best possible way.

All his life, Rav Tzvi's *kibbud av va'eim* was exceptional. He became a famous *maggid shiur,* and sometimes his proud father would enter the beis midrash a bit late to listen to his son's *shiur.* Rav Tzvi would interrupt the *shiur* to take care of his father. He would run to help his father to his seat, and hand his father his own gemara so that he could follow along. (Someone would run to bring Reb Tzvi another gemara.)

During the first eleven months after a parent passes away, it is a great mitzvah for his sons to lead the *davening* on weekdays. During the year following the passing of Rav Tzvi's father, there was only one time when he did not lead the davening. And it was not his fault.

It was at Shacharis at Bnei Brak's Itzkowitz shul, known as a "*minyan* factory." That's because there are many *minyanim* there for Shacharis, Minchah, and Maariv all through the day and much of the night. For Shacharis, there are *minyanim* from early morning until the latest time one is still allowed to *daven* Shacharis according to halachah. The shul is like a factory in that it is "producing" *minyanim* for much of the day and night.

One morning, Rav Kowalsky was standing near the *amud* so that he could lead the *davening* at the next *minyan,* which would be that morning's last *minyan* for Shacharis. And then he heard the voice of an elderly man:

"I can't walk home by myself. Can someone walk me home?"

This man had just finished Shacharis. He was hoping that someone who had *davened* at the same *minyan* would come forward to walk him home. But no one did. It seems that they were all in a hurry to get to work and did not have the time to walk him home.

A few minutes passed and the old man's voice could be heard once again. "I can't walk home by myself. Can someone walk me home?"

Rav Kowalsky, who by now was standing at the *amud,* turned around. No one was offering to walk the man home. He approached the old man and said in his friendly way, "Come; I would be happy to walk with you." He took the man's hand and they slowly made their way to the apartment building where the man lived.

When they arrived in front of the building, the elderly man thanked Rav Kowalsky warmly, but Rav Kowalsky was not finished. He wanted to complete the mitzvah, so he accompanied the man up the stairs to the door of his apartment.

When Rav Kowalsky returned to shul, the last *minyan* had already begun, so he could not serve as *chazzan*. That was the only time he did not lead the *davening* in memory of his father in the eleven months after his father's passing.

That night, his father appeared to him in a dream. "Tzvi," his father told him, "it is fine for you not to serve as *chazzan*, as long as you do such mitzvos instead!"

His Mother Gets a Crown

It was an amazing scene. People were on their feet, applauding with tremendous excitement. Everyone seemed to have the same feeling — that the announcement that had just been made would change the course of Jewish history.

It happened at the Knessiah Gedolah, the first world conference of Agudas Yisrael, which was held in Vienna, Austria, in 1923. A young Rav named Rabbi Meir Shapiro had addressed the large crowd and announced a new idea that would be known as "Daf Yomi." He suggested that on Rosh Hashanah, which was just a few weeks away, Jews around the world begin to learn one *daf* (two sides) of Gemara a day, beginning with the first *daf* of *Masechta Berachos*, the first *masechta* in *Shas*.

When the Knessiah Gedolah ended and everyone went home, many were wondering, "What will happen on Rosh Hashanah? Will Jews all over the world really begin learning the same *daf*?"

At that time, there were 100,000 Gerrer chassidim in Poland. On the night of Rosh Hashanah after Maariv, the Gerrer Rebbe turned to his *gabbai* and said, "Please bring me a *Masechta Berachos*. I have to begin learning the *Daf Yomi*." Moments later, he was sitting and learning the first *daf* in *Berachos*.

"What mitzvah did you do that our mother should be granted such great reward?"

When the chassidim saw their Rebbe learning "the *daf,*" they did the same. Soon word spread throughout Poland that the Gerrer Rebbe, one of the leaders of the generation, was learning *Daf Yomi.* The day after Rosh Hashanah, every *sefarim* store in Poland sold out its entire stock of *Berachos gemaros*!

Great rabbanim in Eretz Yisrael and other parts of the world were also learning *Daf Yomi*. Rabbi Meir Shapiro's suggestion had become a reality. Who would have dreamed at that time that almost one hundred years later, close to 100,000 Jews would fill MetLife Stadium on a cold winter day to celebrate the completion of the thirteenth cycle of *Daf Yomi*! And around the world, hundreds of thousands of other Jews celebrated as well.

Rabbi Meir Shapiro had a sister who lived in Romania. She knew nothing about her brother's speech at the Knessiah Gedolah. The only way she communicated with her brother in Poland was by mail. A few weeks after Rosh Hashanah that year, Rav Meir received a letter from his sister.

Dear Meir:

On the night of Rosh Hashanah, I dreamed that I saw our mother in Gan Eden and she was wearing a beautiful crown. Tell me, my dear brother, what mitzvah did you do that our mother should be granted such great reward?

"Because My Father Told Me"

Rabbi Dovid Trenk was a very beloved *menahel,* rebbi, and friend. And he was also a very wonderful son to his parents.

For many years, his mother worked in Manhattan and went home by subway. It was very convenient because the train stopped only a few blocks from her house. Very often, Mrs. Trenk would come out of the subway station to find her son Dovid sitting in his car, waiting for her. He had arranged his schedule that day so that he could be at the station when his mother came off the train and drive her home.

When Rabbi Trenk was almost eighty, he became ill with a terrible disease that eventually took his life. Though the illness made him very weak, he tried his best to do as many mitzvos as possible.

Though he was ill, he still wanted to do it the way his father had told him.

When he was no longer able to go to shul, he *davened* at home. One morning after he finished *davening* Shacharis, Rabbi Hillel Brull came to visit. Rabbi Trenk had taken off his *tefillin* but had not yet wound the *retzuos* (straps). In order to put the *tefillin* back in their velvet case, the *retzuos* must be wound around the box in which the *tefillin* are kept.

Rabbi Trenk asked Rabbi Brull to wind the *tefillin* for him and explained why he could not do so himself. "When I was 14 years old, my father visited me at Camp Munk and saw that I was winding the *retzuos* while I was sitting down. He told me that not only should I put on the *tefillin* while standing (which is the halachah according to Ashkenazic custom for both the *shel yad* and *shel rosh*), but I should even stand while winding the *retzuos* and putting the *tefillin* away. But today I don't feel strong enough to stand anymore. So please wind the *retzuos* and put away the *tefillin* for me."

Rabbi Brull was happy to do so, but he did not understand. "Rabbi Trenk, I am sure that your father [who had passed away long ago] would be *mochel* if, at this point in your life, you sat down to wind the *retzuos*."

"It's not a question of being *mochel*," Rabbi Trenk responded. "I know that my father would not be upset with me if I sat. All his life, my father never raised his voice to me, never showed any anger. But I still want to do it the way he told me. So please do it for me."

When Rabbi Trenk's sons became bar mitzvah, he taught them the way his father had taught him, to wind the *retzuos* and put away the *tefillin* while standing.

Gone, But Never Forgotten

The Steipler Gaon, Rabbi Yaakov Yisrael Kanievsky, did not have an easy life. When he was eleven years old his father, Reb Peretz, passed away. A short while later, some

The Steipler Gaon found a most beautiful way to honor his parents.

bachurim from the Novarodok Yeshivah came to his town seeking *talmidim* for a new Novarodok branch that was being opened for young boys. Yaakov Yisrael's mother, Rebbetzin Brachah, made a painful decision. She knew that her son had outgrown the local *cheder* and she understood that he had the potential to become a great *talmid chacham.* So with a heavy heart, she allowed him to travel far away from home to join this new yeshivah. From then on, she and her dear son would see each other only a couple of weeks a year, when Yaakov Yisrael returned home for Succos.

Many years later, the Steipler found a most beautiful way to honor both of his parents. He named his *sefer* on Chumash *Bircas Peretz,* with the word *Bircas* representing the name of his mother, Brachah, and the word *Peretz* for his father. In the introduction to that *sefer,* he writes that he was fulfilling a teaching of *Chazal,* "Honor them when they are alive, honor them when they have passed away" (*Kiddushin* 31b).

A Minyan and a Meeting

"Daniel, is everything set for your trip?"

Daniel Steinberg's* suitcase was packed as he was about to leave on a business trip. His schedule for the next two days had been carefully arranged.

There was only one thing that was still undecided: Where would he *daven* Shacharis?

He would be staying at a hotel right where he needed to be. The problem was that the nearest Orthodox shul was an hour's drive from there — and it had only one *minyan* at six-thirty a.m. That meant he would have to be up at five, and he usually had a hard time getting out of bed. There were times when he would go on a business trip and *daven* in his hotel room. He knew that this was not the right way, but he just could not get up so early — or so he thought.

This time, though, there was a special reason why he wanted to *daven* with a *minyan.* It was within the first eleven months after his father passed away. A son should try to be the *chazzan* on weekdays during those months, and even if he does not lead the *tefillos,* he should say the *Kaddish* at the end of *davening.*

Right before he left, Daniel made his decision. *There's no way I'm not going to shul. Saying Kaddish is a big zechus for my father. I'm not going to give up this zechus.*

Sure enough, the first morning of his trip, Daniel was up by five o'clock and was in his car by five-thirty. He arrived at the shul on time and was the *chazzan* for Shacharis.

"*Yasher koach* for leading the *davening,*" a voice called out to Daniel when Shacharis ended. "Michael Rothschild's my name. I noticed on your *tallis* bag that your name is Daniel Steinberg. Are you by any chance related to Reb Nota Steinberg?"

"Yes, he was my father. That's why I was *chazzan* and said *Kaddish* after *Aleinu.*"

"He passed away? I'm so sorry! I knew your father well — he was such a special person."

"Well," replied Daniel, "it's really amazing that I'm in this far-out place on business and I meet someone who knew my father. That makes me feel good."

Mr. Rothschild was silent; he seemed to be thinking about something. "You know," he finally said, "our organization, the Chofetz Chaim Heritage Foundation, will soon publish a book called *Chofetz Chaim — A Lesson a Day* on the laws of *lashon hara.* Each lesson is to be learned on a specific day of the year, and people donate money to our organization to dedicate a lesson in memory or in honor of someone.

"I want to dedicate one day in memory of your father. I'll give you my secretary's number and she'll tell you which dates are still available so you can choose one. Most of the dates have already been sold."

Daniel was very touched by this kind offer. As soon as he returned from his trip, he called Mr. Rothschild's secretary, who was expecting his call. "Yes, Mr. Rothschild told me that we're giving you a free dedication in memory of your father. Well, you are very fortunate because we still have one date open — all the others have already been sold.

"So that's the date you'll have to take. It's... " and she proceeded to tell Daniel the one Hebrew date that was still available.

When Daniel heard the date, he almost dropped the phone. It was the date of his father's *yahrtzeit*!

He had made a special effort to *daven* with a *minyan* for the sake of his father's *neshamah,* and Hashem had arranged that he honor his father in yet another meaningful way.

At the Top of the Pile

Over the years, Rabbi Chaim Kanievsky received tens of thousands of letters from all over the world, most of

Rav Chaim made a special pile for writers who had his father's name.

them asking him a question on some Torah topic or requesting a *berachah* for something. Rav Chaim always responded.

When responding to the letters, he would first sort them into different piles. There was a pile of letters sent by Kohanim, so that he could honor Kohanim by responding to their letters first. And then there was a pile of letters sent by Leviim.

About seventeen years after the passing of his great father, Rav Chaim started to make a new special pile — of letters whose writers were named Yaakov Yisrael, his father's name. He explained that it was very likely that these writers had been named after his father, who was one of the greatest Torah leaders of his time. Therefore, by responding to their letters before the others, he was honoring his father!

A Reason to Be Happy

Jonathan Rothman* woke up with a start. For the fifth time in the past two weeks, he had the same dream.

It was not a bad dream — but what did it mean?

In the dream he saw his father, who had passed away many

years before. Each time, his father appeared to be very happy. But he did not say anything. What was it that made him so happy?

Jonathan told the dream to his family, to his friends, to his business partners, even to his doctor. No one could explain the dream to him.

He was a very wealthy man. He was willing to pay any amount of money to know what the dream meant. But no one could help him.

One day, Jonathan passed by a shul. He had an idea. "I'm not religious," he thought, "but I know that rabbis are wise people. Maybe the Rabbi of this synagogue can tell me what the dream means."

Soon he was sitting in the Rav's office telling him about the dream. When he finished, the Rav said, "I don't know what the dream means, but I have a suggestion. In Israel, in the city of Bnei Brak, there is a great Rabbi, one of the greatest in our generation, who might be able to help you. His name is Rabbi Aharon Leib Shteinman. I could arrange for you to meet with him, and you can tell him about your dream."

Jonathan arranged to take a three-day trip to Eretz Yisrael.

"It was like offering food and drink to a starving person."

Soon after his arrival, he was sitting in the small, very simple apartment of the *gadol hador,* Rav Aharon Leib. With the help of an interpreter, Jonathan described his dream. When he finished, Rav Aharon Leib sat in silence for a few minutes, thinking. Finally, he said:

"Tell me, do you use your money to do kindness for others?"

"Well," Jonathan replied, "I do give charity, to Jews and to non-Jews."

"In recent weeks," Rav Aharon Leib then asked, "have you done anything special with your money?"

Jonathan did not have to think very long. "Yes. Though I'm not religious, I'm a proud Jew, and I know that the Talmud is very meaningful to the Jewish people. Recently, someone told me about a new edition of the Talmud being printed in Israel that would have special diagrams in the back to make it easier to understand the different cases being discussed. They were looking for sponsors for the printing costs. It seemed to me that this new edition will help students to better understand the Talmud and would be a very good thing for the Jewish people.

"So," Jonathan concluded, "I donated $150,000 toward the printing of these... 'gemaras,' I think they're called."

Rav Aharon Leib smiled. "I think we have the answer. Let me ask you a question. If a father is starving and terribly thirsty, and his son comes forward to offer him food and drink, do you think the father would smile at that son? Of course he would!

"Your father has been very 'hungry and thirsty' in the Next World. He cannot do any good deeds there; he needs *you* to do good deeds because that will help him in the Next World. When you gave $150,000 for those gemaras, it was like offering food and drink to a starving, thirsty person.

"Your father is very grateful for what you have done. And that is why he comes to you in dreams and appears happy."

Part 2
Halachos

Halachos

Halachah 1:
The Basics

We must be very careful to honor our father and mother by assisting them whenever possible (kibbud), and to always show proper respect for them (yirah).

The Gemara says that *kibbud av va'eim* is a challenging mitzvah. It is challenging because it applies every hour, every day, every year. From the time we are young until we are old, we must honor our parents. And we must honor them throughout *their* entire lives.

I once went into a store where an elderly man was sitting behind the counter. The elderly man was the store owner's father. The owner was doing what he thought was a great mitzvah. His father could no longer work, but it was good for him to keep busy. So the son asked his father if he would sit behind the counter and help out.

But what I saw was not good. It got busy in the store and the father was giving a customer incorrect information. The son got upset and spoke sharply to his father. There is no excuse for this. If the son could not control his feelings, it would have been better for him not to ask his father to sit behind the counter.

A Delicious, Terrible Meal

The Gemara says that a person can serve his father or mother a delicious meal and be punished by Hashem for it! It tells the story of a man who served his father a fattened bird, something that rich people ate in those days. The father was touched that his son had gone to such expense and asked his son, "How could you afford to prepare such a meal for me?"

The son's reply was shocking. "Old man, what do you care (how I was able to pay for it)? Just chew and eat!"

Whatever reward the son might have earned for preparing such a meal was canceled by the terrible way he spoke to his father. Perhaps he spoke that way because he had a hard day and was very tired and stressed. But that's no excuse. A child must always speak respectfully to his father or mother.

Acting With Respect When We're Very Close

Another reason why we have to be very careful with *kibbud av va'eim* is because children are so close with their parents. When we are very close with people and comfortable with them, we tend to treat them as friends.

Many students become very close to their *rebbi* or *morah*. But we can never "kid around" with a *rebbi* or *morah* the way we would with a friend.

And the same is true with a parent. When you're shopping with your friend for a new hat and your friend asks, "Does this look good on me?" you might respond jokingly, "Yes, if looking like a gangster is considered looking good." But you should not say that to a parent.

Waiting for the Right Moment

A man once came to Rabbi Moshe Feinstein very distressed. Something unpleasant had happened in his family and his twelve-year-old son, upset over what had occurred, said to him, "Daddy, it's all your fault." These words hurt the father very much.

Rav Moshe felt that the boy was too young to understand just how wrong and hurtful his words were. But twenty-five years later, in a private moment, Rav Moshe told him, "Twenty-five years ago when... you said..." He explained to him that even if his words were true, it is absolutely forbidden to talk that way to a father, and he suggested that the young man ask his father to forgive him.

Rav Moshe waited twenty-five years to tell the man to ask his father for forgiveness.

Halachah 2: **Help in a Pleasant Way**

What is considered giving honor to a parent? One must give him (or her) food or drink, dress and cover him, bring him in and take him out. And he should do this in a pleasant way.

You might be thinking, "I should bring my father or mother food? But my mother brings *me* food! She's a great cook and serves me great meals whenever I'm home!"

Well, for starters, you can help serve the meal, and in doing so, serve your father or mother. If you are old enough and your mother trusts you alone in the kitchen, then every once in a while you can suggest that your mother sit like a queen at the table while you serve the meal.

And there is something even simpler that you can do. If the family is sitting around the table enjoying a meal together and your father or mother says, "Please pass the water pitcher," then do even better. Take the pitcher and instead of passing it, pour the drink for your father or mother. And you can do even more; if you notice, for example, that your mother's glass is empty, offer to pour a drink for her before she asks that you pass the pitcher.

If your mother asks you to go to the grocery store to buy some food items, have in mind that by doing so, you are fulfilling the mitzvah of *kibbud av va'eim*. Make sure to carry out your errand in a cheerful way, not with complaining or in any way that shows unhappiness.

We have offered a few suggestions. You can surely think of more!

Just the Way He Liked it

Rabbi Avrohom Genichovsky was exceptional in the way he performed mitzvos, including *kibbud av va'eim*. He knew that his father enjoyed a hot glass of tea at the end of his meal. Once, when he knew that his father would be attending a *yahrtzeit seudah* in a certain shul, Rav Avraham arranged for someone to serve his father a glass of tea at the end of the *seudah*.

Halachah 3:
Endless Opportunities

There are many ways — too many to mention — to honor our parents.

Rambam points out that when *Shulchan Aruch* (and the Gemara) says that we honor our parents by helping them with their food or clothing, these are just some examples. There are many, many other ways to honor them.

When Peninah* became a *kallah,* her mother mentioned how special she was even as a child. "Peninah was seven years old," said her mother, "when her younger sister was born. The day I came home from the hospital with the baby, I was tired and pretty weak. But there was no adult at home to help me; my husband was at work and could not leave early. I came downstairs to prepare supper for the children — and was I surprised! Peninah had set the table and had done a very good job. She saved me some *koach,* and the mere fact that she had done this for me gave me strength."

Halachah 4:
Greeting Our Parents

Greeting a parent is a sign of honor and respect. If your father or mother is standing among a crowd, make sure to say "Hello" to them before greeting anyone else.

Chazal tell us that a *chassan* is compared to a king and a *kallah* to a queen. It should follow, then, that if a boy attends a wedding, the first person he should greet is the *chassan;* a girl should greet the *kallah* first.

However, Rabbi Chaim Kanievsky is quoted as saying that we *always* greet our parents before anyone else. If, for example, you are coming to the wedding from sleepaway camp and you haven't seen your parents in a while, make sure to greet them first.

Visiting Day is eagerly awaited by campers everywhere. In one summer camp, the moment learning sessions ended on Visiting Day morning, campers would line the road to watch as the cars pulled into the parking lot.

"David, you seem very anxious. What time did your parents say they're coming?"

David,* a nine-year-old camper, did not respond. He did seem quite anxious. Finally, the moment arrived — he recognized his parents' gold Volvo coming down the road. He began jumping up and down with excitement. "They're here! They're here!" he shouted.

The car pulled into the parking lot and out stepped David's father and mother... followed by Barky, the family dog. David ran toward his parents, his arms outstretched, and as they met he embraced... Barky.

After that incident, each year on Visiting Day morning following Shacharis, the head counselor would tell the campers, "Boys, for these four weeks that you're away from home, you and your parents don't see each other. Make sure you greet them as soon as you see them, and show them proper respect and appreciation throughout the day."

Halachah 5: **Standing Up for a Parent**

Just as it is a mitzvah to stand up in respect for a talmid chacham, so too it is a mitzvah to stand up in respect for a father or mother.

It is common for parents to be *mochel* and tell their children they don't have to stand up for them. However, Rabbi Shmuel Kamenetsky, America's senior Rosh Yeshivah, says that it is a "beautiful *hanhagah*" (behavior) for children to honor their parents by standing up for them. Rav Shmuel encourages *rebbeim* and *moros* to teach this halachah to their students.

Even when parents are *mochel,* if you are lying on a couch reading a book and your father or mother enters the room, it is proper to at least sit up as a sign of respect.

A Reason to Sit

There was excitement in a shul in Yerushalayim. A *bris* would be taking place there, and the *gadol hador,* Rabbi Elazar Menachem Shach, was coming from Bnei Brak to be *sandak.*

Finally, someone announced, "The car bringing Rav Shach has arrived! He will be entering the shul momentarily."

"Quick, everyone — sit down!"

It was the voice of none other than Rabbi Sholom Mordechai Schwadron, the famed Maggid of Yerushalayim.

What did he mean? Why did he tell everyone to sit down?

Realizing that some people did not understand, he explained, "If Rav Shach walks in and we're all standing, then we don't get a mitzvah. But if when he enters we are seated and then we stand

"The car bringing Rav Shach has arrived!"

up to honor him, we have done the mitzvah of standing up to honor a *talmid chacham*."

Reb Shach entered the shul and everyone stood up in his honor.

Rabbi Chaim Pinchas Scheinberg grew up in America, became a Rosh Yeshivah there and then moved his yeshivah, Torah Ore, to Yerushalayim. He was one of the *gedolei hador* until he passed away in 5772 (2012) at age 101.

There was an elderly Kohen living near Torah Ore who would *daven* Shacharis in the yeshivah. In Eretz Yisrael, *Bircas Kohanim* takes place every single day. Rav Scheinberg would try to quickly sit down after *Bircas Kohanim* ended so that he could have the mitzvah of standing up for this elderly man when he passed by on his way from the *aron kodesh* back to his seat. When Shacharis ended, Rav Scheinberg would ask a *talmid* to bring this man a cup of coffee.

Once, Rav Scheinberg grabbed a *talmid's* hand and pulled him to sit on a bench with him. "Rebbi, what's going on?" the

Rav Scheinberg stood up to show the elderly Kohen respect.

talmid wondered. He did not have to wait long to figure out what was happening. The yeshivah's *mashgiach,* Rabbi Zeidel Epstein, was about to pass by, and Rav Scheinberg wanted his *talmid* to join him in the mitzvah of standing up for this *talmid chacham* and tzaddik. This is truly amazing when we consider that Rav Scheinberg was the Rosh Yeshivah and around the same age as Rav Epstein! Rav Scheinberg stood up for Rav Epstein because he knew that it was a mitzvah to show him respect.

Halachah 6: ***Whom to Honor First***

If your father says, "Please bring me a drink," and at the same time your mother says, "Please bring me a drink," you should bring your father his drink first.

It's important to stress: *The mitzvah to honor a mother is just as great as the mitzvah to honor a father.* It is because of certain obligations that a wife has to her husband that the halachah requires us to serve our father before our mother.

The Gemara says that a man should honor his wife more than himself. Very often, when a man will hear his wife ask for a drink just after he asked for one, he will tell his child, "Serve Mommy first." Of course, if this is the father's wish, the child should fulfill it and serve his mother first.

Tzaddikim are very sensitive toward the feelings of their wives.

A Reason to Return

Rabbi Aharon Kotler was the founder and Rosh Yeshivah of Beth Medrash Govoha in Lakewood, New Jersey, but he lived in Boro Park, Brooklyn. *Talmidim* would take turns driving Rav Aharon to and from yeshivah.

One day, a *bachur* named Chaim Reisman had the privilege of driving the Rosh Yeshivah from Boro Park to Lakewood.

"I'm so sorry, Chaim, but we have to go back. I forgot something."

They had been on the road for about half an hour when Rav Aharon said, "I'm so sorry, Chaim, but we have to go back. I forgot something."

Chaim knew that if the Rosh Yeshivah wanted to go back home it must be important. He immediately turned the car around and headed back to Boro Park.

A half-hour later, they pulled up in front of the building on Fifteenth Avenue where Rav Aharon and his rebbetzin lived. Chaim said to his rebbi, "The Rosh Yeshivah can stay in the car. I will get the Rosh Yeshivah whatever it is that he forgot."

"Thank you, Chaim," Rav Aharon replied, "but this is something that I need to do myself."

They both got out of the car, entered the lobby of the apartment building, and began to climb the stairs. When they reached Rav Aharon's apartment, he knocked on the door and his rebbetzin opened it, surprised to see her husband standing there.

"A gutten tog" ("Have a good day"), he said to his rebbetzin with a smile.

"A gutten tog," she replied.

With that, Rav Aharon turned around and headed down the stairs. He had returned to Brooklyn because when he left the first time, he had been preoccupied and had forgotten to say goodbye to his rebbetzin.

When Reb Chaim Reisman told this story years later, he added, "From the look of joy on the Rebbetzin's face it was obvious that it was well worth the extra hour of driving for Rav Aharon to return to Brooklyn."

When Each One Asks for the Other

What if one's father asks him to bring his mother a drink at the same time that his mother asks that he bring his father a drink? Should he listen to his father, because honoring a father comes first, or should he listen to his mother because she is telling him to honor his father?

Rav Yitzchok Zilberstein answered this question with a famous teaching of *Chazal*: רְצוֹנוֹ שֶׁל אָדָם זֶהוּ כְּבוֹדוֹ, *To fulfill a person's wish is to honor him* (see *Yerushalmi Peah* 1:1). Since it is the father's wish that his child bring a drink to the mother, that is what the child should do.

A similar story happened in the home of Rabbi Chaim Pinchas Scheinberg.

In their old age, Rav and Rebbetzin Scheinberg always had someone in their apartment with them during the daytime to help them with their needs. One day, Rav Scheinberg called their assistant, who happened to be Rav Scheinberg's *talmid,* into his study. At the same moment, the Rebbetzin called to the *talmid* from a different room; she also needed something. The *talmid* felt that since Rav Scheinberg was his rebbi, he should go to him first.

"What does the Rebbi need?" he asked.

"Before we get to that," said Rav Scheinberg, "did I hear the Rebbetzin calling you?"

"After you take care of her, come back to me."

"Yes, Rebbi."

"Then please go see what she needs. After you take care of her, come back to me."

The *talmid* headed to the Rebbetzin.

"What can I do for the Rebbetzin?" he asked.

"Before we get to that," she replied, "I think I heard the Rosh Yeshivah calling you — is that right?"

"Yes, Rebbetzin, he did call me."

"In that case," she said, "first take care of the Rosh Yeshivah, then please come back to me and I'll tell you what I need."

Halachah 7:
Their Seats at the Table

We are not allowed to sit in the chair at the table that has been designated as our parent's chair. This means we cannot sit at the spot at the table where they usually sit, and we cannot sit in their designated chair even if we move it to a different spot.

For many years, I had the good fortune of living only a few blocks from my parents, Reb Shmuel Avigdor and Mrs. Selma Finkelman. On Erev Shabbos, I would come with my children to wish "Bubby and Zeidy" a good Shabbos (and to partake of Bubby's famous chocolate chip cookies). Sometimes other children and grandchildren were there as well, and the kitchen would get crowded. Very often, my mother would get busy with her cooking and tell me or one of my siblings, "Sit in my seat." Since my mother was instructing us, we obeyed and sat in her chair at its regular spot at the table.

There was something that all of us noticed. Even if my father was resting and was not in the kitchen, and even though she knew that my father would not mind, my mother *never* told any of us to sit in my father's chair. This was because my father and mother always treated each other with great respect. My mother was willing to be *mochel* where her own *kavod* was concerned, but not for my father's *kavod.*

My father was a quiet man and did not demand much from his children. But he had a firm rule at the Shabbos *seudah.* "No one can start eating until Mommy sits down." We did not begin eating the next course — whether it was fish, chicken, dessert, or anything else — until our mother had finished serving and was seated at the table. Of course, if my mother would say, "Your soup is going to get cold — start eating," he would allow us to do so. But only if Mommy gave permission.

My father retired at an early age because he developed a problem with his feet that made walking very difficult. My mother had a full-time job at a nursing home six blocks from their home. She knew that it was hard for my father to be alone all day, so she would walk home every day during her lunch break so that they could eat lunch together.

When my mother came home at the end of her workday, she would find a snack on the kitchen table and hot water ready for her coffee, lovingly prepared by my father, who had limped around the kitchen to get everything ready for her.

Halachah 8:
No Contradicting

It is forbidden to contradict a father or mother.

"Esti, don't put the cup so close to the edge — it can fall off the counter and break!"

"Mommy, don't worry so much. It's not close to the edge."

"The music at last night's wedding was way too loud — as usual. I'm going to tell my sister that next time she makes a wedding, she should put out earplugs for guests who want to use them."

"Ta, actually the music wasn't loud at all. I don't think you should tell Aunt Leah anything."

In both of these examples, the child has been guilty of contradicting the parent. If a mother says that the cup is too close to the edge, the child cannot say that it isn't. What Esti could have said is, "I'm so sorry Mommy, I didn't realize it was so close to the edge."

In the second example, the boy could have said, "Ta, I don't mean to be disrespectful, and I know how much loud music disturbs you... but compared to most of today's weddings, the music last night was really not loud. I'm afraid that if you say something to Aunt Leah, she might feel hurt."

It's important to always keep in mind: It all depends how we say it. The same idea can be said in a way that is respectful or in a way that is disrespectful. This is true not only when speaking to parents. Shlomo HaMelech says, "The gentle words of the wise are heard" (*Koheles* 9:17). When we speak gently and respectfully, it is much more likely that people will listen to what we are saying and take our words seriously.

Rav Pam's mother was warmed by her father's words throughout her long life.

Rabbi Avraham Pam would share a story that happened with his mother, Rebbetzin Rochel Leah Pam, when she was nine years old.

Rochel Leah decided that she would not eat or drink the entire fast of Asarah B'Teves. She knew that her father, the Rav of the city of Shedlitz (Poland), and her mother would never allow her to do this. So she spent the entire day at the homes of friends. After dark, when the fast was over, Rochel Leah came home.

"Rochel Leah," her father asked, "have you eaten anything today?"

"No," she answered quietly.

One of the important townspeople had come to speak to the Rav and was in the room when this conversation took place. He should have kept quiet and let Rochel Leah's parents deal with what happened, but he decided to voice his opinion. "If this *fasteger* (one who was fasting) was my child... oh, would she get it, this *fasteger...*"

Rochel Leah's father did not answer the man, Instead, he and his wife took their daughter into the kitchen and served her supper. When she finished eating, she went straight to bed. A few minutes later, her father came into the room.

He took her into his arms and said very gently, "Rochel Leah, *mein kind* (my child), Mommy and I know that you meant to do a mitzvah today when you fasted. But you should know, it is not a mitzvah for a nine-year-old to fast. *B'ezras Hashem* when you are bas mitzvah, then it will be a mitzvah for you to fast.

"Now, my child, I'm sure that you are very tired from a day of fasting. Sleep well, my child, sleep well."

When Rebbetzin Rochel Leah Pam was ninety years old, she said that she was still warmed by her father's words whenever she thought about what happened on that night many years before.

Halachah 9:
No Endorsing

A child is not allowed to say that he agrees with what his father or mother has said, unless his father or mother asks for his opinion.

A father says, "A person should not borrow money unless he has a plan for paying it back."

His son says, "I agree with you, Daddy. How can a person borrow without knowing how he's going to pay it back?"

The son should not have said that.

You might be wondering: "I can understand that it's wrong to contradict my father. But what's wrong with agreeing with him?"

Well, imagine that you are on line to ask advice of Rabbi Chaim Kanievsky *zt"l*. You ask your question and Rav Chaim tells you his answer. The man behind you on line, who heard the question and the answer, says out loud, "I agree with what Rav Chaim said. You definitely should listen to him."

People would stare at this man in shock. They would be thinking, "You're telling us that you agree with Rav Chaim? Are you implying that you are equal to him, that his words need your endorsement? That is very disrespectful of Rav Chaim, the *gadol hador*!"

When we say that we agree with what our parents have said, we give the impression that we consider ourselves equal to them — and that is disrespectful.

It is important to know that according to *Sefer Chareidim*, a basic part of *kibbud av va'eim* is to view our parents as very special people. Very special people do not need our approval or endorsement.

Rabbi Avraham Pam once said that truthfully, every Jew is a special person, and not only because he is a member of Hashem's Chosen People.

The Mishnah says, "Do not look down at any person... because there is no person who does not have his hour" (*Avos* 4:3). Every Jew has his moment in life when he does something great and shows the true worth of his *neshamah*. Rav Pam would illustrate this point with a story:

> *Rav Pam's mother had a Jewish housekeeper who worked hard to eke out a living. One day, a friend mentioned that she needed three hundred dollars for something very important, but did not have the money. The housekeeper said, "You know what? I'll lend you the money." She lent her three hundred dollars — which was all the money she had saved up over much time! She had emptied out her savings to help a friend.*
>
> *Unfortunately, the friend passed away suddenly before paying back the loan. Rav Pam's mother walked alongside her housekeeper at the levayah and heard the housekeeper whispering, "I am mochel (forgive) you... I am mochel you." Instead of crying over her lost money, the housekeeper was worried that her friend would be judged in Shamayim for borrowing money and not paying back. So she made sure to say clearly at the levayah, "I am mochel you..."*

That, said Rav Pam, is the sort of greatness that even so-called "simple Jews" are capable of.

No Questions Asked

My wife's grandfather, Mr. Jacob (Jack) Freeman, was born near Boston over a hundred years ago. His parents were deeply religious but there were no yeshivos for young Jack to attend. Even so, he grew up to be religious like his parents and was usually early for *minyan*. He kept Shabbos, kashrus, and all the other mitzvos although, through no fault of his own, he was never able to learn Torah.

When Jack graduated high school, he decided that he wanted to become a lawyer. His parents were thrilled with his choice. Lawyers were highly respected and usually earned a lot of money, which the family had not had very much of until then.

Jack had to attend college for four years before he could move on to law school. Things were going smoothly until the beginning of one school term. Jack received his schedule of classes and saw that one of his required courses would be given on Friday night.

Jack lived within walking distance of the college, so getting there and back on Shabbos would not have been a problem. He did not have to write during this class; all he had to do was be present and listen to what the teacher was saying.

It seemed that there was no *chillul Shabbos* involved. But was it right to attend a college class on *Shabbos Kodesh*?

Jack decided on his own that attending a college class was not something that he should be doing on Shabbos. He would not take that course.

But he could not go on to law school without that course.

So he quit college and became a carpenter. He earned a fraction of the money that he could have earned as a lawyer and did hard, physical work instead of sitting behind a desk.

"One never knows what incredible zechusim are found even among pashute Yidden."

When I married my wife, she did not know this story because her grandfather was a quiet man and did not like talking about himself. The story became known when my wife's grandparents were honored at their shul's annual dinner. Before the dinner, the shul's Rabbi, Rabbi Yehudah Kelemer, visited Mr. and Mrs. Freeman and asked that they tell him about themselves. That is when Mr. Jack Freeman told the Rabbi his story.

At the time of that dinner, I was a student at Beth Medrash Govoha in Lakewood. When I told my Rosh Yeshivah, Rabbi Shneur Kotler, the story of how my wife's grandfather gave up his dream of becoming a lawyer and instead became a carpenter, all for *kavod Shabbos,* he exclaimed, "One never knows what incredible *zechusim* are found even among [so-called] *pashute Yidden* (simple Jews)."

Halachah 10:
Learning Torah

In regular conversation, we are not allowed to argue with parents or contradict them. Discussing Torah with one's father is different. The way of learning Torah is to discuss, debate, and argue. When a father learns Gemara with his son, he wants his son to argue with him if, for example, he feels that the Gemara means something else. But even then, the son must be careful to express himself in a respectful way. He should never say to his father, "That doesn't make any sense!" or "My rebbi would never say such a pshat."

The rule is: Argue, but with great respect at all times.

A Time to Speak Softly

"Wow, Rabbi Moshe Feinstein, the *gadol hador,* is here at the wedding," Gavriel* said to a friend. "I think I'm going to ask him the *kasha* that I asked Rebbi in *shiur* today."

"The one that had Rebbi stumped?" his friend Ari responded.

"Yes."

The two *bachurim* quickly made their way over to the Rosh Yeshivah before anyone else did. They greeted him and Rav Moshe responded with a warm smile. "May I ask the Rosh Yeshivah something I asked in *shiur* today?" Gavriel asked.

Rav Moshe nodded, and Gavriel proceeded to ask his question.

Rav Moshe knew all of *Shas* by heart and did not need to be told the details of the topic. Gavriel named the *masechta* and the *daf,* and then asked his question.

"We don't speak to a rebbi the way we speak to a chavrusa."

Rav Moshe immediately responded with a clear, brilliant answer.

But Gavriel was not completely satisfied with the answer. "But according to what *Tosafos* are saying, it would seem..."

Rav Moshe calmly explained how his explanation *did* take into account what *Tosafos* say.

Gavriel, however, was still not satisfied. He argued with what Rav Moshe had said. But that wasn't all. Gavriel was really getting excited, as people often do when they argue in learning. He was shouting at Rav Moshe. The problem was, Gavriel wasn't arguing with his *chavrusa* in yeshivah. He was arguing with an older person, a *talmid chacham,* who happened to be the greatest of the generation.

People were watching and were quite upset. No one was sure what to do. It seemed that each time Gavriel responded to what Rav Moshe said, his voice was raised even more.

Rav Moshe, who was amazingly humble, decided that he had to teach Gavriel a lesson that was more important than understanding the Gemara they were discussing. As the Mishnah says, "If there is no *derech eretz,* there is no Torah" (*Avos* 3:17).

Rav Moshe gently put his hand on Gavriel's wrist and the boy abruptly stopped talking. Quietly but firmly, the *gadol* said, "We don't speak to a rebbi the way we speak to a *chavrusa.*"

Gavriel understood and he lowered his voice.

Halachah 11: **Don't Ignore**

It is disrespectful to ignore a parent's instructions.

"Rochi, it's cold outside — make sure to put on a sweater."

"Mordy, that shelf is not so strong. Don't put any more *sefarim* on it."

If Rochi does go out without a sweater or if Mordy puts one more *sefer* on that shelf, he or she has not fulfilled the mitzvah of *morah av va'eim,* to have great respect for our father and mother, as the Torah says: אִישׁ אִמּוֹ וְאָבִיו תִּירָאוּ, *Every man shall have great respect for his mother and father* (*Vayikra* 19:3).

But what if Rochi is really not cold and will be uncomfortable if she has to wear a sweater? She could say, "Mommy, I don't mean to be disrespectful, but I really don't feel cold. Would it be okay if I skipped the sweater this time?" If her mother replies, "I understand, but I'm afraid you'll catch a cold — please put it on," then Rochi should definitely try to wear it.

If Mordy needs to put that *sefer* away and can't find room on any other shelf, he could say, "Abba (or Daddy), I understand that you're afraid the shelf will break. Where do you suggest I put this *sefer*?"

Anyone feels bad when their words are ignored. To ignore what a father or mother says is very disrespectful.

A Time to Eat

The Imrei Emes of Ger, Rabbi Avraham Mordechai Alter, loved to learn Torah. Even as a young *bachur,* he would spend his days and nights immersed in the sweet waters of Torah.

One night, he was riding a train, learning from a *sefer* the entire time. Late at night, he looked at his watch, quickly closed his *sefer,* and took out a package of food. A man sitting nearby watched as young Avraham Mordechai ate what was in the package, recited a *berachah acharonah,* and then took out his *sefer* and resumed learning.

"What was that all about?" the man wondered. "I've been sitting across from that *bachur* for a few hours and the whole time, he did not eat or drink anything. All he did was learn. And then late at night, he checks his watch and begins to eat! Is he in some sort of contest and is timing himself to see how long he can wait before he eats?

"I know it's not my business, but I'm so curious, I have to ask him."

The man approached the *bachur.* "Young man," he said, "can you explain to me why you did not eat anything until late at night, after you checked to see what time it is?"

The Imrei Emes made sure to obey his mother's instructions.

Avraham Mordechai replied quietly, "When I left home this afternoon to head for the train station, my mother gave me a package of food. 'Make sure you eat it today,' she told me. For many hours, I forgot to eat, but then I suddenly remembered. I checked my watch and saw that it was not yet morning. When my mother said to eat it 'today,' I think she meant to finish it by the end of the night. I quickly ate the food so that I could do as my mother instructed."

A similar story is told about Rabbi Chaim Kanievsky. When he was a *bachur* learning in Petach Tikvah, he would come home every Shabbos. His mother wanted to make sure that he had nutritious food to eat, so she would prepare a package for him to take back to yeshivah each week. Young Chaim was so absorbed in his learning that many times he would forget about the package. By Friday morning a lot of food was still left, some of it no longer very fresh. Chaim knew that when he got home, his mother would ask, "Chaim, did you make sure to eat everything that I sent?" Chaim would never lie, and he did not want his mother to be upset. So each week before he headed home, he made sure to finish all the food that was left.

"I Didn't Mean That!"

It was a difficult time in Eretz Yisrael. There had been a number of terrorist attacks in and around Yerushalayim, and people had been hurt. Some people were changing their schedules so that they could be home more of the time and in the street less.

One of those who did *not* change his schedule was Rabbi Shmuel Aharon Yudelevitch. (He was a son-in-law of the famed tzaddik Rabbi Aryeh Levin and a brother-in-law of the *posek hador* Rabbi Yosef Shalom Elyashiv.) Rav Shmuel Aharon began his day before dawn when he arose to prepare to *daven* at a *minyan Vasikin*. He would arrive home in the evening after *davening* Maariv following a day filled with Torah, *tefillah,* and *chesed.* He placed his trust in Hashem that He would watch over him as he went about his *avodas Hashem* in the way that he had since his youth.

Then one day, he received a letter from his mother, who lived in Northern Israel, in the town of Kfar Tavor:

Dear Shmuel Aharon:

I have read about the terrible terrorist attacks in Yerushalayim. May Hashem watch over acheinu Bnei Yisrael wherever they are. Shmuel Aharon, I am very worried about you since I know that you get up very early and go to sleep very late. I assume that when you walk the streets of Yerushalayim in the early morning hours and late evening hours there are not many people in the street. I am afraid for you to be out walking alone. It seems that to be in the streets alone in such times is more dangerous. Shmuel Aharon, please don't leave your house during nighttime hours. Daven in the morning when it is already light outside and make sure to be back in your house before dark.

Be well. Best regards to Rasha and the children,
Mama

Rav Shmuel Aharon was terribly upset by this letter. On the one hand, he wanted very much to follow his mother's words. On the other hand, all his life, he had tried to do every mitzvah in the best possible way. He had been *davening* Shacharis at a *minyan Vasikin* since before his bar mitzvah. And as for Maariv, though we are allowed to *daven* Maariv before sunset, the preferred time is after dark when we can also fulfill the mitzvah of *Shema* in its proper time.

What was he to do?

Rav Shmuel Aharon thought the matter through and came to the conclusion that since his mother was asking him to *daven* Shacharis and Maariv in a way that was not ideal, he was not

The thought that he was not fulfilling his mother's wishes gave him no rest.

obligated to obey her. It is possible that he felt that since he had been *davening* this way for so many years, it was considered a *neder* (vow), and one is not allowed to go against a *neder*.

One thing is certain: Rav Shmuel Aharon's greatness in Torah and fear of Hashem were outstanding. If he decided that he could continue to *daven* as he had always done, then he knew that this was correct.

Even so, the thought that he was not obeying his mother's wishes gave him no rest. His children saw that he was not himself.

"What's wrong, Tatte?"

"What's wrong? I'm going to shul when it's still dark, as I always do. But I know that Bubby would not be happy if she knew I was doing so."

Someone had an idea. He wrote a letter to Rav Shmuel Aharon's mother, telling her that Rav Shmuel Aharon was very distressed because of what she had asked of him. His mother was not surprised that her son was still *davening Vasikin* in the morning and Maariv after dark. She knew very well how important every mitzvah was to her dear son. She was not happy to hear that her letter had upset him so much, though she was touched that he had taken her words so seriously.

Soon, Rav Shmuel Aharon received another letter:

> *Dear Shmuel Aharon:*
>
> *I hear that you are upset because you are not obeying my request. Please understand: I was not* ***insisting*** *that you leave your home only when it is light outside and return while it is still light. It was only a* ***suggestion*** *that you do so. If you feel that you must continue to daven at the time that is ideal, I fully understand and respect that.*
>
> *Be well, my dear son. And may Hashem continue to watch over you.*
>
> *Love,*
> *Mama*

After reading the letter, Rav Shmuel Aharon's joy was indescribable.

Halachah 12: ***"Why Me?"***

When a father or mother asks a child to do a chore, he should not respond, "Why me? I always get stuck with these jobs! Why can't someone else do it?"

This is a disrespectful response. If a child truly feels that he is given more chores than his siblings, he could speak to his parent privately and say, for example, "I don't mean to be disrespectful, but I was wondering why Baruch or Chaya can't take out the garbage. I may be wrong, but I think the last three times, I was asked to do this job."

If the parent responds, "Please take out the garbage now and we'll discuss this later," the child should obey.

If the parent says, "I'm not discussing it. Do as you were told," the child should still obey. That is the halachah.

It is interesting that the halachah says that a parent should not make life overly difficult for a child. As Rabbi Shmuel Kamenetsky pointed out, when a parent makes unreasonable demands, there is the possibility that the child will not listen and then the parent will be guilty of transgressing וְלִפְנֵי עִוֵּר לֹא תִתֵּן מִכְשֹׁל (*Before a blind person do not place a stumbling block* — *Vayikra* 19:14), which forbids us from causing another Jew to sin.

Parents should try to figure out what they can request from each particular child so that their requests will be honored and appreciated. And children have their mitzvah, to obey their parents even when it is not easy.

"Why Me?"

"Yoni, I need you to bring in the groceries from the car so I can start preparing supper."

"Mommy, why me? Why do I always get stuck with these jobs? The other kids never get asked to do these things. It's always me. It's not fair!"

Yoni hadn't noticed, but his father had come home from work as his mother was asking him to help. Yoni's father heard his response and was not happy. Instead of speaking to Yoni directly, he tried something else.

"Children, after Yoni brings in the groceries, I want everyone to sit down at the table. There's something I'd like to tell you." A few minutes later, he began.

> *Children, let me tell you a story about myself.*
>
> *You know that I'm a Holocaust survivor. When the Germans entered our town, they rounded up all the Jews and brought us to the local train station, where two trains were waiting to leave. An officer announced that we were to file past him and he would direct us to the train we would be boarding. We had no idea that this officer was conducting a selektzia (selection) that was usually done after the prisoners arrived at*

the concentration camp. The train on his right was for able-bodied men who would be sent to work in a slave labor camp. The train on the left was for those considered unfit for work. They would be taken directly to the gas chambers upon their arrival at the camp.

My father was directed to the right. My mother and all of the children were sent to the left. We had no idea that we were being sent to a concentration camp. We boarded the train and my mother started to rummage through her bundles looking for some food when her hand felt something made of velvet.

"Oh, no!" she exclaimed. "Tatty's tefillin! He forgot to take them with him when they separated us!"

My mother turned to me, her oldest child, handed me the tefillin bag, and said, "Yitzy, run quickly across the platform to the other train. Tatty is in the car right across from ours. Give him the tefillin and quickly come back."

I was very frightened. I thought to myself, "Go across the platform to Tatty's train? There are Germans on the platform with guns. We were warned not to leave our train. What will happen if they see me?

"But Tatty needs his tefillin," I told myself, "and Mommy asked me to go. How can I ***not*** *go?"*

I ran across the platform, boarded the other train, found my father, and handed him the tefillin. He gave me a hug and I turned to leave... as the doors of the train closed. And the train began to move...

My mother and all my siblings met their deaths in the gas chambers. I spent the war years in a labor camp; that is how I survived.

"And so, children," Yoni's father concluded, "I am alive today because when my mother asked me to do something that I really didn't want to do, I did it. I didn't ask, 'Why me?'"

Halachah 13
Following Instructions

When a father or mother tells a child to be home by a certain time, the child should make every effort to do so.

A boy might be going to a friend's bar mitzvah. Before he leaves the house, his mother says, "Donny, you've been going to sleep very late. It's getting harder and harder for you to get up in the morning. Make sure that you're home tonight by 9:45 at the latest."

Donny's best response: "Yes, Mommy, I'll be sure to be home by then."

Donny could also say: "Mommy, I understand that you're worried about me, but I don't think anyone else plans to leave the bar mitzvah that early. Would it be okay if I came home at 10:15?"

Donny should *not* say: "What? 9:45! No one else will leave the bar mitzvah so early! Why am I always the only one who gets treated like a baby?"

Such a response is very disrespectful.

A Scare That Should Not Have Been

Mr. and Mrs. Sheinritz* were quite concerned. Their daughter Leah's school day ended at three o'clock. It was now five-twenty and Leah was still not home. They called a few girls who went on her school bus, who said they had seen Leah in school but did not notice her on the bus. Her parents then called the principal, who spoke to the building manager, and a search of the entire school building was conducted. Leah was nowhere to be seen.

Finally, at six o'clock, two hours after Leah should have come home, her parents called the police. A detective soon arrived at their home and was taking down information about Leah.

Suddenly, the front door opened and in walked Leah. Her

mouth opened in shock as she saw her parents at their dining room table looking very concerned, while a man wearing a badge was writing something on a clipboard. Leah quickly figured out what was happening and burst into tears. She had never intended to cause her parents such worry.

Where had she been for the past three hours? At the house of a friend who lived not far from their school. They had walked to the friend's house as soon as school ended and had spent an enjoyable afternoon together. Leah meant to call her parents to make sure that it was all right for her to go to her friend's house, but somehow she had forgotten to do so.

Children should realize that their parents think about them all the time. When a child is supposed to be home by a certain hour and is not home by that time, parents worry. Always call your parents to let them know that you will be home late that day.

Halachah 14:
How to Ask

If a child needs his father or mother to do something for his benefit, he has to be careful to make his request in a respectful way.

It was the "big night" — Gilah V'Rinah High School was putting on their annual play, and Chaya had a leading role. There had been a last-minute play meeting that afternoon; now, Chaya was running late.

Suddenly she remembered that part of her costume was at the cleaners — and the store closed in fifteen minutes!

"Mommy," she said breathlessly as she ran into the kitchen, "I need you to go to the cleaners right away — my blouse and kerchief have to be picked up and the store is closing very soon!"

"No problem, Chaya, I'll drive there right now."

Fifteen minutes later, Chaya's mother returned from the

cleaners with the clothing. "Oh, thanks so much, Mommy! Just put it down on the sofa. I'll take it when I'm ready to leave."

It might not seem that Chaya has said anything wrong. After all, she did have a performance that night, and surely her mother wanted her to look her best! And she did thank her mother.

Even so, a child has to be careful when making requests of a father or mother.

We should not give the impression that our parents are there to serve us. When Chaya said, "Mommy, I need you to go to the cleaners right away," it sounded as if her mother is working for her and she has now given her mother instructions. What she should have said is, "Mommy, my blouse and kerchief for tonight's performance are at the cleaners — and they're closing soon. Do you think it would be possible for you to pick them up for me?"

When Chaya's mother arrived home with the blouse and kerchief, Chaya would have been best off taking them from her (along with a big "Thank you") and putting them on the sofa herself. If she was too pressed for time to do that, she might have said, "Mommy, thanks so much. I really feel bad bothering you but I'm in a great rush — is it possible for you to leave the blouse and kerchief on the couch?" It was wrong for her to say, "Just put it on the couch," which sounds like she is giving her mother orders.

Similarly, a boy should not say to his mother, "I need you to wash my pants." It is better to say, "Can you wash my pants?" And the preferable way is to say, "My pants are dirty. May I put them in the hamper? Are you doing laundry today?"

And when sitting at the supper table, rather than saying to your mother, "Can you pass the salt?" it is better to say, "Mommy, can you please pass the salt?" The second way is more respectful.

Halachah 15: **Always Follow the Torah**

One should not obey his father or mother when told to do something that the Torah does not permit.

The very same *pasuk* that commands us, אִישׁ אִמּוֹ וְאָבִיו תִּירָאוּ, *A man shall revere his mother and father,* continues with וְאֶת שַׁבְּתֹתַי תִּשְׁמֹרוּ, *And you shall keep My Shabbosos* (*Vayikra* 19:3). Why are these mitzvos taught side by side? To teach us, says Rashi, that although we are commanded to have great respect for our parents, we should not obey them if they ask us to be *mechallel Shabbos* or do anything else that goes against our holy Torah.

A father tells a son, "I heard that there was a big argument in shul this afternoon. You were there, weren't you? So who was arguing with whom?" The son cannot offer this information because to do so would be to speak *lashon hara.*

The son should say to his father in a respectful tone of voice, "I don't mean to be disrespectful, but is it possible that I would be speaking *lashon hara* if I were to tell you the names of those men?" If the father were to respond, "I don't think it's *lashon hara,*" the son could say, "Again, I don't mean to be disrespectful, but I think I learned that it is *lashon hara.*"

Usually, if the child speaks to his parent in private and with respect, the parent will appreciate his child's words and will not be angry.

The following story happened in my parents' home when we children were young: My brother came home from yeshivah and told my mother in a very respectful way that according to what he had learned in yeshivah, she needed to change her way of transferring the hot chicken soup from the pot to the soup bowls on Friday night. My mother was happy that her son wanted to do at home what he had learned in yeshivah, and immediately changed her way of serving the soup.

A few days later, my brother came home from yeshivah and said that he had misunderstood his rebbi. In fact, my mother had been serving the soup correctly all along! My mother was not upset at all. She simply went back to her old way of serving.

If we speak with respect, our parents will not become upset.

A Shabbos to Remember

Shuvu is the network of Torah schools in Eretz Yisrael founded by the beloved Rosh Yeshivah, Rabbi Avraham Pam. Many of the students of Shuvu come from homes where the parents do not keep mitzvos — or at least, didn't until their children became students at Shuvu.

For many of these children, keeping Shabbos in a non-religious home is a great *nisayon* (test).

Mazal, a Shuvu graduate who today is the proud mother of two adorable children, related:

> *I come from a home that was non-religious. Thankfully, my parents heard good things about the Shuvu schools and sent me to Shuvu–Tel Aviv.*
>
> *During my third year at the school, one of my teachers invited me to spend Shabbos with her in Bnei Brak. That Shabbos changed my life. It was so beautiful, so special! I decided that I too wanted to keep Shabbos.*
>
> *But that was easier said than done. Our family was "traditional," which means that we did certain Jewish practices, but also did not do many. For example, my father would say Kiddush every Friday night, but after Kiddush my family would turn on the television. After that Shabbos in Bnei Brak, I no longer watched television on Shabbos.*
>
> *On Shabbos afternoons, my family would drive to my grandmother's house for our weekly visit. After that Shabbos in Bnei Brak, I would walk for forty-five minutes to my grandmother's. This meant walking forty-five minutes each*

Shabbos morning in any weather — cold, rain, or blazing sun — so that could I visit my grandmother together with my family, who would drive there in ten minutes.

I did something else for the sake of Shabbos. I spent time creating games and fun activities during the week so that by the time Shabbos came, I would be able to entertain my younger siblings in a way that did not involve any chillul Shabbos.

Baruch Hashem, my parents allowed me to transfer to Bais Yaakov Holon for seventh and eighth grades, where all the students kept Shabbos and all other mitzvos. From there I continued on to Nesivos Rivkah Bais Yaakov High School. As time passed, my father and mother gained more appreciation for the way I was living my life and they actually were very proud of me.

And then it happened. The first Shabbos of my ninth-grade school year, my parents had a big surprise for me. As I prepared to leave on my lonely walk to my grandmother's home, my mother met me at the bottom of the stairs with a proud smile lighting up her face. For the very first time, in honor of Shabbos, my family was going to join me in walking to Savta!

I cannot describe the joy I felt on that glorious Shabbos morning as we walked together. I felt the special kedushah that I had felt on that first Shabbos in Bnei Brak. I realized that you can feel the kedushah of Shabbos wherever you let it in.

Now, just a few short years later, my entire family is shomer Shabbos. My mother recently started dressing according to the laws of tznius and even wears a sheitel. My younger brothers attend Yeshivat Yam Shel Shlomo on Moshav Chemed. As for myself, I graduated seminary in Ofakim and I currently work as a kindergarten teacher in Shuvu–Bat Yam."

Thank You, Hashem, for being with me through all the difficulties. And thank you to my parents for allowing me to choose the path I wanted and for joining me so that we can experience this beautiful life together.

The Letters That Changed His Life

"Rebbi, I don't know what to do. Every time I try speaking with my father, he ignores me."

Michael* was from a non-religious home. His parents had sent him to an Orthodox day school in their city, but they did not want him to become religious. They sent him there because they knew that the environment in the day school and the kind of children who attended it were very much to their liking.

In seventh grade, Michael had a rebbi named Rabbi Shmuel Kaufman. Rabbi Kaufman inspired his students to love Torah and mitzvos. By the time Michael finished seventh grade, he knew that he wanted to be religious and he wanted to go to an Orthodox Jewish high school after eighth grade.

His mother was not happy about this, and his father was furious. "What do you need those old-fashioned laws for? Why do you have to study those books? You're smart and a great ballplayer, Michael; you can be anything — a rocket scientist or a baseball pitcher. Come to your senses and stop this religious stuff!"

As much as it hurt Michael to see his father so upset, he knew that in Torah and mitzvos, he had discovered the truth. He was a mature, confident boy. He was going to live a religious life and he was going to continue learning Torah.

In eighth grade and with his rebbi's help, he was accepted into a mesivta high school for the coming year. His father told him, "Michael, I had enough of this insanity. You're a big boy and I'm not going to force you to go to a school that you don't want to attend. But this is the last time I'll ever speak to you. As far as I'm concerned, you're not my son."

Michael was very hurt. The next year, he lived in the dormitory at yeshivah and would call home at least once a week. If his father answered the phone, he would hand the phone to Michael's mother without saying a word.

Before he left for yeshivah, Michael spoke to his rebbi. "It's so painful to me that my father won't talk to me. Is there anything that I can do?"

"Yes, Michael, there are two things that you can do. One is to *daven* that your father should have a change of heart and welcome you back as the good son that you are. The second thing that you can do is write letters to your father."

"Letters? What's the point? He probably won't read them anyway. And what should I write?"

"I don't know if your father will read the letters, but it makes no difference. You have a mitzvah of *kibbud av.* Writing to him is fulfilling that great mitzvah. As far as what to write, you should always begin by saying that you love him, that you are thinking of him, and that you hope that he is well. And then you can write about something from the week that just passed."

Michael, now Michoel, accepted his rebbi's instructions and wrote a letter to his father every week — for ten years. He did not receive a single letter back. Not a phone call. Nothing. But he continued to write and to *daven*.

He married a fine young woman and studied in a kollel. His mother took ill and passed away. His father was living alone. He continued to write to him.

And then it happened.

Michoel's phone rang. "Michael, it's Dad. Michael, I'm so lonely. Do you think I could come and stay by you for a little while?"

"Of course, Dad, of course! You're always welcome. I'll come to pick you up this evening."

For years, it seemed that Michoel's letters had not accomplished anything at all. But when his father felt so lonely after his mother passed away, he remembered those letters and realized that he had a son who still loved him. He was not alone.

Michoel's father lived with him and his family for the rest of his life. Slowly, he began doing some mitzvos; eventually, he kept them all. He even began learning Gemara.

And all because his son never stopped trying to be a son.

Halachah 16: **Playing Sports**

A son or daughter must be very careful when playing sports with a parent.

They cannot "play rough."

They have to be careful to speak respectfully, even in the heat of the game.

The Torah states that it is a terrible sin for a child to intentionally strike a parent, causing him to bleed or become black and blue (see *Shemos* 21:15). For this reason, a child should avoid any situation where he might cause his father or mother to bleed unnecessarily, or to become black and blue.

Someone who is diabetic must draw a drop of blood at least once a day to check his sugar level. Very often, elderly parents need someone to prick their skin and draw the blood for them. The *poskim* rule that it is preferable that a child not be the one to draw the blood, because he or she might mistakenly draw a bit more blood than necessary. If there is no one else to do it, a child may draw the blood since this is for the parent's health.

Is there anything wrong with a father and son playing sports together? Is there concern that the son might injure his father, causing him to bleed or get bruised?

Rabbi Shmuel Kamenetsky, Rosh Yeshivah of the Philadelphia Yeshivah, had this to say:

> *Sports is considered an enjoyable activity that father and son can do together. An important part of a parent-child relationship is the bond formed by doing enjoyable activities*

together. For some, playing sports together can be one of those activities.

Even though injuries do happen when playing sports, most of the time people do not walk away injured when playing a sports game. Since in most cases there is no injury, therefore there is no concern according to halachah. However, if it is a game where some sort of injury or bruise is very probable, it should be avoided.

In other words, fathers and sons should not play tackle football or a rough game of basketball together. When playing basketball, a son should be careful not to foul his father, as this could cause a bruise or other minor injury.

Children have to be careful to speak respectfully, even in the heat of the game.

A son should not argue with his father over a call.

Certainly, he should not laugh or make fun when his father makes a bad play.

Of course, we should *never* make fun of or laugh at *anyone* who makes a bad play. To make fun is to act with very poor *middos.* And when arguing over a play, we should do our best to stay calm and avoid name-calling or accusing the other team of cheating.

After all, it's only a game. Of course it's nice to win, but our main goal should be that everyone has an enjoyable time. If we keep that in mind, we will always act with respect on the ball field and will surely act toward our parents with respect when playing ball with them.

When playing ball, it would be a good idea to take a lesson from Aaron Shalom Tepfer.

A Different Kind of Win

Aaron Shalom Tepfer was a wonderful boy who lived in Lawrence, New York, and attended Yeshivah Darchei Torah. At age eleven, he died as a result of an accident. Aaron

Aaron Shalom taught by example what's most important when playing a game.

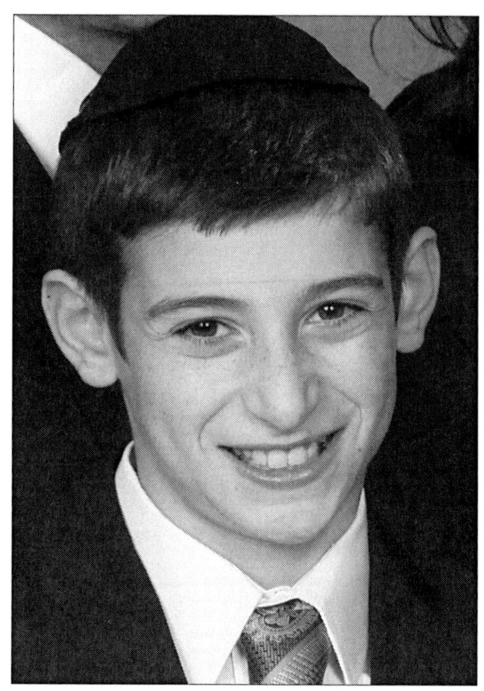

Shalom will always be remembered as a truly special boy who was very sensitive to the feelings of others.

He was very athletic and was chosen to be the pitcher in his team's Little League championship game. It was a very close game. Toward the end of the game, Aaron Shalom asked his coach if another boy could take over the pitching and he would take that boy's position.

"But why, Aaron Shalom?" asked the coach. "You're doing a great job; Dovi* can't pitch as well as you can. Why switch positions?"

"Because I know that he really wants to pitch," Aaron Shalom replied sincerely.

The coach saw that Aaron Shalom was willing to take a chance on losing the game, rather than win the game and have this boy feeling bad that he never got a chance to pitch. The coach agreed to honor Aaron Shalom's request, and the two boys switched positions.

Who won the game? That's not important for us to know. What is important is to remember the lesson that Aaron Shalom taught by example. Even in the midst of a very important game, never forget that what's most important is to treat everyone with respect and sensitivity.

Those who remember this lesson will never act disrespectfully toward their parents on the ball field.

Halachah 17 **A Parent's Name** | ***A child is not allowed to refer to his parents by their first name.***

For example, if someone is asked, "Which of the Cohen brothers is your father?" he may not reply, "Yitzchak." To do so is disrespectful. Even if a parent is *mochel,* we are not allowed to do or say something that is disrespectful.

How should a child respond if he is asked that question? He could say, "Reb Yitzchak," "Dr. Yitzchak," or "Mr. Yitzchak," whatever is appropriate.

An exception to this rule is when a child is *davening* for a *refuah sheleimah* for his father or mother. All Jews are servants of Hashem, so it would not be proper when speaking to Hashem to say "Reb Yitzchak" even for one's father. A child can say, "Please send a *refuah sheleimah* to *avi mori* (my father, my guide), Yitzchak ben Sarah."

What happens if a *gabbai* in shul wants to call his own father to the Torah for an *aliyah*? It would not be proper to say, "*Yaamod* Yitzchak ben Avraham." Some *gabbaim* simply say, *"Yaamod avi mori,"* without saying their father's name. However, because it is customary in most places to call people to the Torah using their names, and some *poskim* insist on this, it is best to say, " *Yaamod avi mori,* Reb Yitzchak ben Reb Avraham."

When someone is asked by a *gabbai* for his full Hebrew name, he has to say his father's name. He should answer, "Yaakov ben *avi mori* Yitzchak" or "Yaakov ben Reb Yitzchak."

A Gentle Correction

In the last years of Rabbi Avraham Pam's life, a *minyan* was held in his home every Shabbos for all the *tefillos*. One Shabbos afternoon at Minchah, Rav Pam was called to the Torah as "Moreinu ('Our Leader') Harav Avraham Yaakov ben Meir HaKohen." Rav Pam was not pleased that he was called "Moreinu" while his father, who was an outstanding *talmid chacham*, was just "Meir" and not even "Reb Meir"!

After *davening*, Rav Pam wanted to say something to the *gabbai* so that in the future he would not make this mistake. To avoid insulting him, he decided to make his point indirectly. Rav Pam said:

"You know, my father was an outstanding *talmid chacham*. He learned *b'chavrusa* with Rav Elchonon Wasserman in the Chofetz Chaim's Kollel Kodashim, and in America he was a distinguished Rav and a *maggid shiur*."

"My father was an outstanding talmid chacham."

The *gabbai* understood why Rav Pam said this and he made sure not to make that mistake again.

Halachah 18 **Choose Wisely**

There are times when because of kibbud av va'eim, we have to do a mitzvah in a way that is correct but not ideal.

Bedikas Chametz — Which Is the Best Night?

"I'm not sure what to do. So I'll ask my rebbi, Rav Pam."

Yitzchak and his wife were preparing to spend the first days of Pesach with her parents in Monsey. He planned to do *bedikas chametz* in their own apartment on the last night they would be home before leaving for Yom Tov. But Yitzchak wasn't sure which night that would be.

He knew that according to halachah, it's best to perform *bedikas chametz* on the night before Pesach, the night which the first mishnah in *Masechta Pesachim* says is the proper time. We recite the *berachah* of *Al Biur Chametz* only if the *bedikah* is done on that night.

But Yitzchak also knew that his mother-in-law was counting on him and his wife to help with the pre-Pesach preparations. If they stayed home until the night of Erev Pesach, they would only be able to help out on Erev Yom Tov. Maybe he should do *bedikas chametz* a night early (without a *berachah*) so that they would have a whole extra day to help his mother-in-law?

To Rav Pam the answer was simple. "It is very important that you help your mother-in-law so she can enter Yom Tov with peace of mind. You should do *bedikas chametz* a night early."

Chanukah Lecht or Erev Shabbos Minchah — Which Comes First?

"A *gutten Erev Shabbos,* Tatty!"

"*A gutten Erev Shabbos,* Menachem! Come inside, everyone — and *a lichtige Chanukah*!"

It was Erev Shabbos Chanukah and Menachem had come with his wife and children to spend Shabbos with his parents. He had arrived late on a short Friday afternoon. He quickly unpacked and got his family settled. Looking at his watch, Menachem realized that if he hurried, he would have just enough time to *daven* Minchah before lighting the menorah. It is best, if possible, to *daven* Minchah on Erev Shabbos Chanukah before the lighting.

He knew that there was a *minyan* only a few short blocks away. He hurried to the shul and was happy to see that he was on time for Minchah. About twenty minutes later Menachem headed back to his parents' home.

"Perfect," he thought to himself. "I'm already dressed for Shabbos. Twenty minutes left until candle-lighting for Shabbos. That leaves just enough time for everyone to light the Chanukah *lecht* before the ladies *bentch Shabbos lecht."*

As he approached his parents' house, Menachem was surprised to see his father standing by the front door looking quite worried.

"Ta, is everything okay?" he asked.

"Menachem... Menachem... where were you?" his father asked.

"Oh, I went to *daven* Minchah before lighting *Chanukah lecht*."

"But, Menachem," his father said, still obviously upset, "Shabbos... what about Shabbos? We have to be ready for Shabbos!"

It was then that Menachem realized that he had made a mistake. His parents never rushed into Shabbos, getting things ready until the last minute. In their home, the table was set and everyone was dressed well before candle-lighting time. His father would spend the hour before Shabbos learning or saying *Shir HaShirim*.

By *davening* Minchah, Menachem had arrived home with just twenty minutes to Shabbos, and the Chanukah *lecht* had not yet been lit. Instead of *davening* Minchah, Menachem should have remained at home and *davened* Minchah in shul after lighting his menorah. This way, everyone could have lit Chanukah *lecht* earlier. Had he done so, his father would have been calm, not upset.

It was a lesson he would never forget.

Yom Kippur — Where Should He Daven?

It was a hard time for Nosson and his mother. Nosson's father had passed away in the summer, and the start of the new year in yeshivah was hard for him. And it was hard for his mother that he was away in yeshivah all week, coming home only for Shabbos. But she knew that for his growth as a *ben Torah,* it was important that he be in the dormitory all week like the other boys.

Knowing how hard it would be for his mother to be alone for two days of Rosh Hashanah, he had *davened* in a shul near their home and spent Yom Tov with her. As Yom Kippur approached, he was faced with a dilemma.

"I know that if I ask my mother's permission to remain in yeshivah for Yom Kippur, she'll tell me to do so. But I also know that it will mean a lot to her if I sleep at home and *daven* nearby.

"I also know that I *daven* so much better in yeshivah.

"What should I do?"

"We never lose out from doing the right thing."

Nosson decided that he would bring his question to the great Ponovezh Rosh Yeshivah, Rabbi Elazar Menachem Shach, and would do as he said.

Rav Shach listened carefully as the *bachur* explained his dilemma. Then he replied, "One thing is for sure — we never lose out from doing the right thing. It seems to me that the right thing would be for you to spend Yom Kippur at home so that your mother should not be alone. I assure you that your *kibbud eim* will not cause you to lose out. You will only gain!"

Halachah 19:
Erev Shabbos and Shabbos

Erev Shabbos and Shabbos are ideal times to show honor and consideration for our parents. We should offer to help and certainly, we should help when we are asked.

"Why is your wet clothing still on the line? It's close to Shabbos, and this place looks like a mess. Take it off already."

"Oh, look who's talking. Mr. Cleanliness is giving *mussar*! You're the one who's always leaving garbage lying around on Friday afternoon!"

The Gemara (*Gittin* 62a) tells of two neighbors who would often get into arguments on Friday afternoon. Then, R' Meir moved into the neighborhood and saw what was happening. He made a special effort to bring peace between these neighbors — and he succeeded! No longer did they fight with one another. R' Meir was able to hear the *Satan,* who tries to incite us to sin, say with sadness, "I'm no longer wanted where I used to be welcome."

Rabbi Avraham Pam said that the *Satan* purposely chose Erev Shabbos to incite these neighbors to fight. Erev Shabbos is a very busy time, and people sometimes get tense as they try to finish their preparations in time for Shabbos.

"Who has the shoe polish?"

"I have no clean white shirts!"

"Why are you taking so long in the shower? There are three more people on line!"

When people get tense, it is easy for them to lose control of their emotions. They grow angry and yell, or say things that hurt people's feelings. That's exactly what the *Satan* wants.

The *Satan* also knows that all the blessings for the next week come from Shabbos, and he does not want us to receive those blessings. So he tries to get us to enter Shabbos in a bad mood and become upset with one another.

We have to learn from R' Meir and let the *Satan* know that he is not welcome in our homes on Erev Shabbos. We have to remain calm and respectful, especially to our parents.

It is good to start preparing for Shabbos early to avoid tense situations.

Imagine that it's an hour before Shabbos and your mother says, "The baby has an infection. I need you to go to the pharmacy and pick up the medicine." You are tempted to respond, "I haven't even started getting ready for Shabbos. Let someone else go. Why do I always have to be the one?"

Halachah does not allow us to respond this way. It would be best not to wait until the last minute to get ready for Shabbos. One reason is that being ready at least a few minutes early shows *kavod* for Shabbos and allows us to enter Shabbos in the proper mood. Another reason is that an emergency might come up, and someone who is not ready for Shabbos might feel that he cannot help out and also be ready on time for Shabbos.

If you feel that you really don't have the time to run an errand for your mother or father, then you might say, "I really don't mean to be disrespectful, but I'm afraid that if I go to the pharmacy, I might not have enough time to get ready for Shabbos. Is it possible that someone else could go?"

Many people start their Shabbos preparations on Thursday night, or even earlier. Of course, it is wonderful for children to offer to help their mothers on Erev Shabbos instead of waiting for their mothers to ask for help.

At the Shabbos Table

The Shabbos *seudah* is an ideal time to honor our parents and give them *nachas.* When boys come home from shul, they should make sure to wish their mothers "*Gut Shabbos.*" Children should offer to bring food and other items to the table, make sure there are enough chairs, and so on.

Rav Pam would tell his *talmidim* to always come to the *seudah* with a *dvar Torah* that their mothers will understand and appreciate. "Your mothers prepare a beautiful *seudah,*" he would tell them. "They never say, 'This week I'm tired; no *seudah* this week.' No, they never say that. Week after week, they prepare a *seudah* that everyone will enjoy.

"*Bachurim* should come to the *seudah* prepared to add to the *ruchniyus* by saying a *dvar Torah* that everyone will appreciate."

Rav Elyashiv made sure to compliment his rebbetzin for her cooking.

Rabbi Yosef Shalom Elyashiv was a man of few words. And food was not important to him. His mind was always focused on Torah and he ate whatever he was served. But he still made sure to compliment his rebbetzin for her cooking. Sometimes after a Shabbos *seudah,* he would say that the meal was like a feast at the table of Shlomo HaMelech! We should learn from Rav Elyashiv and make sure to thank and compliment our mothers after each meal.

Halachah 20
A Parent's Sleep

It is wrong to disturb anyone's sleep. It is especially wrong to disturb our parents' sleep. For example, on Shabbos afternoon when our parents are napping, we have to be careful not to make noise that might awaken them. On the other hand, it is correct to wake up a parent for a mitzvah if the time for the mitzvah to be done will soon end. If your father is sleeping and you realize that the time for saying Krias Shema will soon end, it is a mitzvah to wake him up.

In the *Stories* section, we tell the story found in the Gemara about Dama ben Nesinah, the non-Jew who would not awaken his father even though this meant that he would lose a fabulous sum of money.

Sefer Yaalzu Chassidim writes that from the story of Dama ben Nesinah we learn how careful we must be not to make noise when our parents are sleeping. Children must be extremely careful to place or receive phone calls, or perform any other noisy activity, only at a time and in a place that will not disturb their parents.

Concerned for Her Father's Learning

For a few years after her wedding, Rebbetzin Chaya Musha was childless. One day, she was feeling especially sad that her home was empty of children.

What does a Jew do when he desperately needs something important? He takes out his *Sefer Tehillim* and pours out his heart to Hashem. And that is exactly what Rebbetzin Chaya Musha did.

"I am going to *daven* my very best," she told herself. "And in my pain, I will very possibly start crying and saying the *pesukim* in a loud voice. But my father is here learning and my *davening* might disturb him."

She thought of a simple solution. "I'll go down to the cellar and say *Tehillim* there. It's damp and musty down there, but this way I won't disturb my father's learning."

She went downstairs, opened her *Tehillim,* and began to pray. Before long her tears began to flow. As her *davening* became more intense, so did her sobbing.

Her father, Rabbi Shlomo Elyashiv, known as the Baal HaLeshem (after his *sefer* on Kabbalah, *Leshem Shevo V'Achlamah*), stepped out of his room for a moment and heard her crying. He went down to the cellar and asked what was wrong. She told him how she had been feeling especially sad that day and had decided to pour out her heart in *tefillah.*

"But why are you saying *Tehillim* here in this damp cellar?" he asked.

"Because I didn't want my crying to disturb your learning," she explained.

Her father was very moved. Even in the midst of her pain, his daughter was thinking about his Torah learning. He told her, "I bless you that in the merit of your concern for my learning at a time of such sadness and pain, you should be granted a child within the year."

"In the merit of your concern for my learning, you should be granted a child within the year."

Less than a year later, she gave birth to a boy. His name was Yosef Shalom Elyashiv and he became famous throughout the world as a *posek* and leader of his generation.

Awakening a Tzaddik

Sefer Chassidim (which was written by Rav Yehudah HeChassid, one of the *Baalei Tosafos*) states: "It is a mitzvah to awaken one's father to go to the *beis haknesses* [to pray] or for some other mitzvah."

"Saba, please wake up!"

"Saba" was Rabbi Sholom Mordechai HaKohen Schwadron, known as the "Maggid of Yerushalayim."

Toward the end of his long life, Rav Schwadron was quite ill and was hospitalized. When his condition improved and the doctors said that he could be released, his family decided that he could no longer live alone in his apartment in Yerushalayim. (His rebbetzin had already passed away.) He was taken directly from the hospital to his daughter's home in Bnei Brak.

He arrived there exhausted. After being served a small meal,

Rav Schwadron was helped to a bed, where he fell into a deep sleep.

The next morning, his daughter told her son, "Saba has been sleeping for a very long time. It would be good for him to *daven*, eat breakfast, and then sit outside in the fresh air. Please wake him up."

The boy entered the room and called softly, "Saba, *boker tov* (good morning). It's time to get up."

Rav Schwadron did not stir. He was sleeping very soundly.

The boy called out in a loud voice that it was time to get up, but Rav Schwadron still did not stir.

His grandson now became worried. Maybe there was something wrong? Maybe his saba wanted to get up but was not able to?

The boy began to move the blanket and make some noise, but his grandfather still did not budge.

Becoming more frantic by the minute, the boy tried blowing into his grandfather's ear, but even this did not cause Rav Schwadron to budge.

"Ima, Ima," the boy ran into the kitchen shouting. "Something is wrong. No matter what I do, Saba is not waking up."

His mother did not seem worried. "Come," she said, "I'll show you how to wake up Saba."

She entered the bedroom and said in a loud voice, "Abba, it's time to say the *Krias Shema* of Shacharis! It's getting late!"

Immediately, Rav Schwadron opened his eyes, lifted his hands, and pushed back the blanket that was covering him. Slowly, he eased his legs off the bed until he was sitting. "*Oy, oy!*" he cried out. "It's getting late to say *Krias Shema*? *Oy vey!*"

His daughter replied, "Don't worry, Abba, there is still time to *daven* and say *Krias Shema* on time. But I was afraid that if you slept much longer, it would get too late."

This calmed Rav Schwadron. "Thank you, thank you!" he

Rav Sholom (on right, with his brother-in-law Rav Shlomo Zalman Auerbach) arose like a lion for the mitzvah of Krias Shema.

said with a smile. And he stood up so that he could get dressed and prepare to *daven.*

From then on, he tried his best to *daven* at a local *minyan Vasikin,* just as he had done in Yerushalayim for many, many years. And how did they wake him up? Each morning, someone would come over to his bed and say, "Saba, we're going to *Vasikin.*" Rav Schwadron would open his eyes, sit up, and prepare himself to *daven* Shacharis.

Halachah 21: **Grandparents**

It is a mitzvah to honor a grandfather and grandmother.

The relationship between grandparents and their grandchildren is very special. A few years ago, Rabbi Yaakov Bender announced a special project at Yeshivah Darchei Torah, where he is Rosh HaYeshivah. During *limudei kodesh* learning in the first part of the day, each rebbi would set aside a half-hour to allow his *talmidim* to write letters to their grandparents. The yeshivah provided paper and envelopes, stamped the envelopes, and mailed the letters.

Many grandparents later said that they were touched by the letter their grandson had written. Several of them saved the letters.

> *When my son was in first grade, the yeshivah took a picture of each boy holding a toy Sefer Torah. Before mailing it to grandparents, the yeshivah had each boy write a short note on the cardboard frame of the photo.*
>
> *My son wrote, "I love you, Bubby and Zeidy, and I hope that you love me."*
>
> *My parents were very touched by the note. It hung in their kitchen for a very long time.*

It is a great mitzvah to honor a grandparent. And it is certainly a great mitzvah to give them *nachas* by making them feel appreciated and loved.

A Win-Win Situation

The Gemara says that Rav Yochanan would stand up in respect for elderly non-Jews. His reason was, "These people have gone through so much!" (*Kiddushin* 33a).

It is wonderful to sit and talk with grandparents and great-grandparents. Grandparents enjoy spending time with grandchildren, and grandchildren can learn a great deal from their grandparents. There is also so much family history that a grandparent has to share. Sometimes, a conversation can reveal information that might otherwise have been forgotten.

When my grandmother, Mrs. Shaindel Hilsenrath, was an elderly widow, she spent many Shabbosos at my parents' home. In one of our conversations, she told us a story we had never heard before:

The Candle Lady

Zeidy, as you children know, was a chassid of the Chortkover Rebbe, Rabbi Yisrael Friedman, one of the great Torah leaders in the years between the two world wars. After the Rebbe passed away, there was no Chortkover Rebbe for a number of years. His two humble sons had a disagreement — each wanted the other one to be Rebbe! (Eventually, the chassidim convinced the two brothers to both be Rebbes and lead the chassidus together.)

One day, Zeidy and I were walking down a busy street in Vienna, Austria, when we saw a woman, whom we had never seen before, calling out, "Candles for Shabbos! Who wants to buy candles for Shabbos?"

No one was buying candles from her. In fact, people were crossing the street so that they wouldn't have to pass by her! The lady looked a bit scary and people seemed to be afraid of her.

But Zeidy and I felt bad for her. She was trying to sell

It was through the "Candle Lady" that my grandparents met the Skolye Rebbe.

Shabbos candles, and she had no customers. So we bought a few candles. After we paid for our purchase, the "Candle Lady" turned to Zeidy and asked, "Do you have a Rebbe?"

What a strange question! Zeidy, as you remember, did not look at all chassidish. He had a mustache and no beard and wore a regular business suit.

Zeidy answered her question. "Well, I am a chassid, but my Rebbe passed away. Right now, I have no Rebbe."

The "Candle Lady" handed Zeidy a piece of paper with an address on it. "Go to this address," she said, "and you will find yourself a Rebbe."

As Zeidy and I walked down the street, we wondered whether we should go to that address, or throw the paper in the garbage. After all, who was this strange-looking Candle Lady?

We decided to go to the address. That was the first time we met the Skolye Rebbe, Rabbi Dovid Yitzchak Isaac Rabinowitz, a holy tzaddik to whom we became very close. A few years later, after the Nazis marched into Austria, Zeidy helped the Rebbe and his family to escape. Later, when all of us arrived safely in New York, Zeidy became the gabbai of the Rebbe's shul in Williamsburg. When Zeidy passed away, the Rebbe said, "I have lost my best friend."

And all this happened because we felt bad for the Candle Lady.

By the way, we never saw her again.

Yes, we have a lot to learn from speaking with our grandparents!

Halachah 22
To Benefit Their Nesahmos

After a father or mother passes away, it is a mitzvah for their son to recite Kaddish for their neshamah, even if the son is not a bar mitzvah. It is a great mitzvah for a son who is over bar mitzvah to also lead the davening on weekdays.

Heaven Sent

"Attention, passengers. Traffic control has informed me that there is a thick fog over New York and the airports have been closed. We will have to land at Dulles International Airport in Washington, DC."

Four businessmen were flying from Cleveland to New York for a trade show. Their early-morning flight was supposed to land in New York with plenty of time for them to join a *minyan* near the airport for Shacharis.

Now, that would be impossible. "You think we'll be able to find a *minyan* in the airport?" Yoel Friedman asked his companion Moshe Steinhardt.

"Well, we're four. And there's that group of chassidim on the plane who had been visiting their Rebbe in Cleveland. I'm pretty sure there are six of them. So we already have a *minyan*!"

When the plane landed, the ten men approached an airport official and asked if he could arrange for them to *daven* in a quiet corner of the terminal. The gentleman was very respectful of their request and directed them to a corner that was free of foot traffic but was in clear view of people walking by. The men each put on their *tallis* and *tefillin* and began to *daven.*

Moments later, a well-dressed man walked by. He looked very sad. Noticing the *minyan,* he walked over to Moshe and said, "Excuse me, but my father died a few days ago. I'm returning home after attending the funeral. I don't really know how to pray, but I know how to say *Kaddish*. Can I say *Kaddish* for my father at the end of your service?"

"Why, of course!" replied Moshe. "Here, have a seat and I'll tell you when to say *Kaddish*." One of the men actually had with him an extra *tallis* and *tefillin* and helped the man to put them on the correct way.

Toward the end of *davening*, the men motioned to the stranger to recite the final *Kaddish*. As he was reciting it, he burst into tears. When *davening* ended, the man told the others something incredible:

> *As I told one of you earlier, a few days ago, my father passed away. I don't live near any synagogues, and until this morning, I had not recited a single Kaddish. Last night my father came to me in a dream and said, "Robert, I need you to say Kaddish for me — why aren't you saying Kaddish?"*
>
> *I explained to my father that I barely knew how to pronounce the words of Kaddish, and besides, there were no synagogues in my area, so it was not possible for me to recite it. My father asked me, "If you are sent a minyan, will you say Kaddish for me?"*
>
> *I replied that yes, of course I would recite Kaddish if I came upon a minyan.*
>
> *I woke up trembling and tried to put the dream out of my mind. I had a flight to catch, so I got dressed and hurried to the airport.*
>
> *And that's when I met your minyan — the minyan that Heaven arranged so that I could say Kaddish.*

Halachah 23:
A Mitzvah That Never Ends

Kitzur Shulchan Aruch writes that reciting Kaddish is not the main way to honor a parent after he or she leaves this world. Most important is that the son or daughter live a life of Torah and mitzvos, that their actions create a kiddush Hashem. Every mitzvah that a child does in this world is a zechus for the parent in the Next World.

When doing the mitzvah of *nichum aveilim,* Rabbi Avraham Pam would often say the following:

When I was a young boy in Lithuania, learning in a yeshivah far from home, it was a joyous day for me when a wagon driver passing by brought me regards from my parents. More joyous was when the wagon driver brought me a letter from my parents. And even greater was when the driver delivered a package with not only a letter, but also some kugel that my mother had prepared.

The Kaddish that a son recites for his parents is like the "regards"; the Mishnayos he learns is like the letter; and when, in addition to Mishnayos, he gives tzedakah as a zechus for the parent's neshamah, it is like adding a piece of kugel to the package.

And as *Kitzur Shulchan Aruch* says, *every* mitzvah that a son or daughter does in this world is a *zechus* for the parent in the Next World.

A Surprise Rebbi

Many years ago, a tragedy happened when an Israeli family on vacation in the United States was in a terrible car accident. The father died; the mother was seriously injured, but she and her young children survived.

At the time of the accident, the family was not religious. The woman spent a long time in the hospital recovering from her injuries. During this time, she thought a lot about why we are on this world. She said, "G-d, if I recover, I promise that I and my children will keep Shabbos and all the other mitzvos." She recovered and was determined to keep her promise. Upon her return to Eretz Yisrael, she enrolled her sons in yeshivos and her daughters in Bais Yaakovs.

One day not long after they had become religious, her young son came home from yeshivah in tears. "Ima," he said to his mother, "tomorrow we're going to have a *bechinah* (test) on some very hard Gemara. I don't know the Gemara. I'm going to fail the test!"

"Yaakov," his mother said, "don't worry. Your rebbi knows that you've been learning Torah for only a short time and that you're trying your best. He doesn't expect you to do as well as the other boys.

"Go to sleep. You'll see that everything will be fine."

Yaakov fell asleep, feeling somewhat better but still worried.

The next morning he awoke with a smile. He told his mother, "Last night, Abba appeared to me in a dream. He told me that after we became religious, he was allowed to enter Gan Eden, and there, he is taught whatever Torah I learn in this world.

"He taught me the Gemara, and now I know it."

Yaakov scored 100 on his test.

"Look in My Son's Sefer"

Rabbi Shmuel Baruch Werner is a great *talmid chacham* and the author of *Mishpetei Shmuel* on Gemara. In that *sefer,* he asks a difficult question and does not offer an answer. After his *sefer* was published, he had a very unusual dream.

In the dream, he saw an elderly woman who identified herself as Mrs. Genichovsky, the mother of a famous *gaon,* Rabbi

The sefer he wrote in his mother's memory was very meaningful to her neshamah.

Avrohom Genichovsky, who lived in Bnei Brak. After his mother passed away, Rav Genichovsky wrote a *sefer* called *Cheder Horasi* on *Masechta Horiyos,* in memory of his mother.

In the dream, Mrs. Genichovsky said to Rav Werner, "Why don't you look in the *sefer* that my son wrote in my honor — you will find that he discusses this question of yours!"

When Rav Werner awoke, he wasted no time in opening his copy of *Sefer Cheder Horasi.* Sure enough, Rav Genichovsky raised his question and offered a beautiful answer! When Rav Werner told Rav Genichovsky about his dream, Rav Genichovsky said that what he found most amazing is that from her place in Gan Eden, his mother seemed to be familiar with the contents of her son's *sefer.*

When a child does a mitzvah in this world, he really has no idea how much pleasure this brings to his parent in Gan Eden.

Sources

Part One: Stories

Chapter One

The Sky's the Limit

Otzroseihem Amalei, the collected *shmuessen* of Rabbi Eliezer Turk, compiled by Rabbi Binyomin Ginsburg

Bread of Blessing

Aleinu L'Shabei'ach (ArtScroll/Mesorah)

A Home for the Glass

Coming Home — 20 glimpses from the road of return in modern America (Israel Bookshop)

A Visit to the Kosel

An article by Rabbi Yoel Chonon Wenger published in *The Jewish Observer*

Last Chance (I)

In the Splendor of the Maggid by Rabbi Paysach Krohn (ArtScroll/Mesorah)

Last Chance (II)

Adapted from a piece by Rabbi Y. Katz in *Chayeinu*

A Perfect Shirt

What a Story! by Rabbi Yechiel Spero (ArtScroll/Mesorah)

Chapter Two

Cheer Up!

Reb Aharon Leib by Naftoli Weinberger (ArtScroll/Mesorah)

A Five-Cent Lesson

When the Curtains Part by C.B. Weinfeld (ArtScroll/Mesorah)

A Lesson From Yosef HaTzaddik

The Maggid Speaks by Rabbi Paysach Krohn (ArtScroll/Mesorah)

Packing Our Parachutes

Powerful Moments by Rabbi Yitzchok Hisiger (ArtScroll/Mesorah)

"Thank You" to the Seamstress

Reb Shlomo by Yisroel Besser (Judaica Press)

A Lesson for Life

Agan HaSahar (Reb Avrohom) on the life of Rabbi Avrohom Genichovsky

Chapter Three

A Bar Mitzvah to Remember

Building for Eternity on the life of Reb Moshe Reichman by Yisroel Besser (ArtScroll/Mesorah)

For the Sake of His Learning

Rav Elyashiv by Rabbi Yehuda Heimowitz (ArtScroll/Mesorah)

A Drive That Was Well Worth It

Rabbi Meir Zlotowitz by Yisroel Besser (ArtScroll/Mesorah)

"Gut Voch" and "Goodbye"

A Blazing Light in the Darkness by Avrohom Birnbaum (ArtScroll/Mesorah)

To Bring Them Joy

Otzer Kibbud Av Va'eim

Finding the Right Chair

Shlomie! on the life of Shlomie Gross by Rabbi Shimon Finkelman (ArtScroll/Mesorah)

A "Deal" With the Rain

L'lo Shem (Hebrew) on the life of Rabbi Ben Zion Follman

A Present for His Mother

Reb Moshe by Rabbi Shimon Finkelman (ArtScroll/Mesorah)

And the Winner Is...

Food for Thought, Volume II, by Rabbi Yitzchok Hisiger (ArtScroll/Mesorah)

The Champion

Reflections of the Maggid by Rabbi Paysach Krohn (ArtScroll/Mesorah)

Chapter Four

Even When It's Hard

Rav Nosson Tzvi by Rebbetzin Sarah Finkel and Rabbi Yehuda Heimowitz (ArtScroll/Mesorah)

A Lesson for Life

Daughters of Destiny (ArtScroll/Mesorah)

Derby to the Rescue

Visions of Greatness, Vol. IX, by Rabbi Yosef Weiss (CIS Publications)

The Butcher's Reward

Seder HaDoros, Part III

A Double Portion of Greatness

Reb Moshe by Rabbi Shimon Finkelman (ArtScroll/Mesorah)

Not for a Million

Voices in the Silence by Rabbi Shlomo Zalman Sonnenfeld (Feldheim)

When the Curtains Parted

Rav Pam by Rabbi Shimon Finkelman (ArtScroll/Mesorah)

Chapter Five

A Lesson From Rav Moshe
Reb Moshe by Rabbi Shimon Finkelman (ArtScroll/Mesorah)

Chapter Six

Like a Guest in His Own Home
HaRav Domeh LaMalach by Rabbi C.S. Rosenthal

A Tale of Two Chairs
From a piece in *Yated Ne'eman* by Dovid Lamed

Give Them Nachas
The Life of Rav Shimshon Pincus (Feldheim)

A Question and an Answer
Reb Aharon Leib by Naftali Weinberger and *Orchos Yosher* [English edition] both published by ArtScroll/Mesorah

A Reason to Delay
Oro shel Olam by Rabbi Yosef Eliyahu

Advice From Rav Moshe
Reb Moshe by Rabbi Shimon Finkelman (ArtScroll/Mesorah)

A Strange Discovery
Otzroseihem Amalei, the collected *shmuessen* of Rabbi Eliezer Turk, compiled by Rabbi Binyomin Ginsburg

The Greatest Blessing
Rav Chaim Kanievsky on Chumash by Rabbi Shai Graucher (ArtScroll/Mesorah)

His Mission in This World
The Rebbe on Beacon Street by Rabbi Shimon Finkelman (ArtScroll/Mesorah)

Chapter Seven

"Just Keep Doing Such Mitzvos"
Ana Avda on the life of Rabbi Tzvi Kowalsky

A *Minyan* and a Meeting

Living the Parashah by Rabbi Shimon Finkelman (ArtScroll/Mesorah)

A Reason to Be Happy

Chakimah D'Yehudai on the life of Rabbi Aharon Leib Shteinman

Part II: Halachos

Just the Way He Liked It

Agan HaSahar on the life of Rabbi Avrohom Genichovsky

A Reason to Sit

The Life of Rabbi Chaim Pinchas Scheinberg (Hebrew) by Rabbi C.S. Rosenthal

A Reason to Return

For Love of Torah by Rabbi Shimon Finkelman (ArtScroll/Mesorah)

When Each One Asks for the Other

A Gadol in Our Midst by Rabbi Shmuel Assayag

A Tale of Two Chairs

Piece by Dovid Lamed in *Yated Ne'eman*

A Time to Speak Softly

Reb Moshe by Rabbi Shimon Finkelman (ArtScroll/Mesorah)

"I Didn't Mean That"

In Every Generation by Rabbi Dovid Yudelevich (Feldheim)

"Why Me?"

Aleinu L'Shabei'ach by Rabbi Yitzchok Zilberstein (ArtScroll/Mesorah)

A Shabbos to Remember

A Tzaddik's Vision by Rabbi Shimon Finkelman (Judaica Press)

A Gentle Correction

Rav Pam by Rabbi Shimon Finkelman (ArtScroll/Mesorah)

Yom Kippur — Where Should He Daven?
Orchos HaYeshivah by Rabbi Asher Bergman

Concern for Her Father's Learning
As related by Rabbi Moshe Elyashiv to Rabbi Binyomin Kirschner, author of *The Gadol Hador* on the life of Rabbi Yosef Shalom Elyashiv (Feldheim)

Awakening a Tzaddik
Voice of Truth on the life of Rabbi Sholom Mordechai Schwadron, by Rabbi Yaakov Aryeh Ariel (ArtScroll/Mesorah)

The Candle Lady
One Small Deed Can Change the World by Rabbi Nachman Seltzer (ArtScroll/Mesorah)

"I'll Send You a Minyan"
Around the Maggid's Table by Rabbi Paysach J. Krohn (ArtScroll/Mesorah)

A Surprise Rebbi
Around the Maggid's Table by Rabbi Paysach J. Krohn (ArtScroll/Mesorah)

"Look in My Son's Sefer!"
Agan HaSahar (Hebrew) on the life of Rabbi Avrohom Genichovsky

Glossary

Aleinu — concluding prayer of Shacharis, Minchah, and Maariv

aliyah (pl. *aliyos*) — lit., ascension; when a man is called to the Torah reading

aron kodesh — (in shul) ark where the Torah Scrolls are kept

aufruf — the Shabbos when a bridegroom or boy at his bar mitzvah is called to recite a blessing at the public reading of the Torah; the act of being called to recite a blessing at the public reading of the Torah, esp. of a bridegroom or a boy or his bar mitzvah

b'ezras Hashem — with Hashem's help

baal korei — person who reads the weekly Torah portion aloud on behalf of the congregation

baal teshuvah — one who has returned to the path of Torah and mitzvos

baal tzedakah (pl. *baalei tzedakah*) — one who is a generous donor to charity

bachur (pl. *bachurim*) — teenage boy or young single man

baruch Hashem — lit., *Blessed is Hashem;* thank Hashem; an expression of appreciation of Hashem's goodness

bedikas chametz — search for leaven on the night before Pesach

beis din — a Rabbinical court

beis haknesses — synagogue

bentch (*Chanukah*) *lecht* — [lighting and] reciting a blessing over the [Shabbos or] Chanukah candles

berachah (pl. *berachos*) — blessing

berachah acharonah — an after-*berachah*

Bircas HaMazon — Grace After Meals

Bircas Kohanim — the blessings recited by the Kohanim during a prayer service

bris, bris milah — circumcision

Chachamim — wise man

chametz — leaven, which is forbidden on Pesach

chas v'shalom — Heaven forfend

chassan — groom

chassid — 1. pious man. 2. the follower of a Rebbe

chassidus— chassidic sect

chavrusa (pl. *chavrusos*) — study partner

Chazal — חז״ל, acronym for חכמינו זכרונם לברכה, our Sages of blessed memory *chazzan* — also referred to as *baal tefillah,* one who leads the prayers in the synagogue

chesed — kindness

chillul Shabbos — desecration of the Shabbos

chuppah — lit., marriage canopy; the ceremony held under the marriage canopy to marry the bride and groom

daf — page, usually referring to a page of Gemara

daven (davening) — pray, praying

derech eretz — proper behavior, in particular respect for parents, teachers and elders

dinar (pl. *dinars*)— a coin used in the days of the Mishnah

dvar Torah (pl. *divrei Torah*) — a Torah insight or explanation

Ephod — garment worn by the Kohen Gadol to which the *Choshen* (Breastplate) was affixed

frum — (*Yiddish*) religious; Torah observant

gabbai — 1. the person in the shul who oversees the smooth functioning of the daily prayers. 2. attendant of a Torah leader

gadol (pl. *gedolim*) — Torah leader

gadol hador (pl. *gedolei hador*) — spiritual leader of the generation

Gan Eden — Garden of Eden, Paradise

gaon — Torah genius, someone with a vast and deep knowledge of Torah

gedolim — great Torah scholars; men of greatness; saintly individuals

gemara (pl. *gemaros*) — volume of the Talmud

gut voch — post-Sabbath salutation: "Have a good week."

gut yom tov — "A good yom tov"; what Jews wish one another on their holidays

Hakadosh Baruch Hu — lit., the Holy One, Blessed is He, G-d

hakafah (pl. *hakafos*) — the encircling of the *bimah* seven times on the holiday of Simchas Torah, while dancing with the Torah Scrolls

hakaras hatov — gratitude

hatzlachah — success, "have great success."

Havdalah — lit., *separation;* prayer recited as the Sabbath or Festival comes to an end

Kabbalas Shabbos — the traditional prayer recited at the beginning of the Sabbath service on Friday evening

Kaddish — prayer recited on behalf of the deceased

kallah — bride

kavod — honor

kavod Shabbos — the honor of Shabbos

kehillah — congregation

kiddush Hashem — doing something that brings honor to Hashem; sanctification of Hashem's Name

kinderlach — (*Yiddish*) an affectionate term for children

Klal Yisrael — Jewish people in general; the Jewish nation

Kohen Gadol — the High Priest who served in the Beis HaMikdash

kos — special cup used for a mitzvah such as *Kiddush* or *Bircas HaMazon*

Kos shel Eliyahu — Cup of Eliyahu [HaNavi]; a special cup placed on the Seder table into which wine is poured at some point and which symbolizes our belief that Eliyahu HaNavi will one day come to announce Mashiach's arrival

kosher l'Pesach — kosher for the Passover holiday (free from *chametz*)

Krias Shema — 3 paragraphs of the Torah recited twice daily, beginning with the words *"Shema Yisrael,* Hear, O Israel."

kugel — a pudding usually made of potatoes or noodles

lashon hara — lit., evil speech; derogatory speech; slander; gossip

lecht — lights, especially those lit in honor of Shabbos or festivals

levayah — funeral

limud haTorah — Torah study

limudei kodesh — study of Torah subjects (as opposed to secular studies)

Maariv — the evening prayer service

maftir — final *aliyah* of the Torah reading which is connected to the reading of the *Haftarah*

maggid shiur — Torah lecturer

masechta (pl. *masechtos*) — Talmudic tractate

Mashgiach — dean of students in a yeshivah who oversees their spiritual and ethical development; can also refer to a *kashrus* supervisor

mechallel Shabbos — one who desecrates the Sabbath

mechanech (n.) — male Torah educator

mechanech (v.) — to provide a Torah education

mechilah — forgiveness

melaveh malkah — lit., escorting the queen; the meal eaten after Shabbos in honor of the Shabbos that has just concluded

menahel — principal in charge of a yeshivah's Torah studies department

mesiras nefesh — self-sacrifice

middah (pl. *middos*) — lit., measure, usually referring to one's character trait(s)

Minchah — the afternoon prayer service

minyan — quorum of ten men needed to conduct a communal prayer service

mishloach manos — gifts of food sent to friends on Purim

Mishnah (pl. *mishnayos*) — a passage from the six volumes of Oral Law compiled by Rabbi Yehudah HaNasi

mispallel (noun, pl. *mispallelim*) — one who prays

mitzvah (pl. *mitzvos*) — Torah commandment

mochel — grant forgiveness

mohel — one who performs *bris milah,* circumcision

morah — a woman teacher

mussar — ethical teachings geared toward self-refinement; reproof

mussar shmuess — a lecture on self-refinement

nachas — pleasure, usually from one's offspring

neshamah (pl. *neshamos*) — soul

nichum aveilim — lit., comforting mourners; making a consolatory visit to a mourner

niggun (pl. *niggunim*) — tune; Jewish

tunes or melodies, often sung during special occasions

paroches — the curtain in front of the Torah ark in a synagogue

pasuk — verse in the Tanach or liturgy

posek (pl. *poskim*) — halachic authority

Rebbe — leader of a chassidic sect

rebbi (pl. *rebbeim*) — Torah teacher

refuah sheleimah — lit., a full/complete recovery; a blessing for a complete/speedy recovery extended to an ailing person

Ribbono shel Olam — lit., Master of the Universe, G-d

rosh kollel — leader of a *kollel*

ruach — spirit; enthusiasm

sandak — one who is honored with holding the baby on his lap during a circumcision

Satan — the prosecuting angel

Seder — special meal and religious service conducted in Jewish homes on the first two nights of Pesach (in Israel on the first night)

sefer (pl. *sefarim*) — book containing sacred Jewish thoughts or prayers

Sefer Torah (pl. *Sifrei Torah*) — Torah scroll

seudah (pl. *seudos*) — meal associated with a mitzvah such as a Shabbos *seudah*

seudas mitzvah — a festive meal, characterized by speeches of *divrei Torah,* celebrating completion of a volume of the Talmud or other significant event

Shabbos Kodesh — the holy Sabbath

Shacharis — the morning prayer service

shalosh seudos — the third meal of Shabbos eaten on Shabbos afternoon

Shas — the Talmud

Shechinah — Divine Presence

sheitel — wig

shel rosh — phylacteries (*tefillin*) worn on the head

shel yad — phylacteries (*tefillin*) worn on the arm

sheva berachos — lit., *seven blessings;* 1. the seven blessings recited at a wedding. 2. festive meals, celebrated during the week after a wedding, at which the seven blessings are recited

shidduch — marriage match

Shir HaShirim — *Song of Songs*

shiur (pl. *shiurim*) — Torah lecture

shivah — lit., seven, the seven days of mourning following the passing of a close relative

shmuess (pl. *shmuessen*) — ethical discourse

Shofet — lit., a judge; leader of the Jewish people in the period following the passing of Yehoshua bin Nun and almost until the reign of Israel's first king, Shaul

shtender — lectern

shul — (Yiddish) synagogue

Shulchan Aruch — Code of Jewish Law authored by Rabbi Yosef Caro some five centuries ago

siddur — prayer book

simchah (pl. *simchas*) — lit., joy; joyous celebration, as a wedding or bar mitzvah

Simchas Torah — the festival immediately following Succos, honoring the completion of the cycle of Torah reading for that year

tallis — prayer shawl, four-cornered

prayer shawl with *tzitzis,* worn during morning prayers

talmid (pl. *talmidim*) — Torah student

talmid chacham (pl. *talmidei chachamim*) — Torah scholar

Talmud Yerushalmi — the Jerusalem Talmud

Tanna (pl. *Tannaim*) — Sage whose opinion is cited in the Mishnah

techiyas hameisim — Revivification of the Dead

tefillah (pl. *tefillos*) — prayer

tefillin — phylacteries

Tehillim — Psalms

Tosafos — 1. critical and explanatory notes on the Talmud by French and German scholars of the 12th–14th centuries. 2. The authors of those notes, collectively

tzaddekes — righteous woman

tzaddik (pl. *tzaddikim*) — righteous man

tzedakah — charity

tzitzis — fringes worn by Jewish men on four-cornered garments

tznius — modesty standard in speech, behavior, and dress

Vasikin — praying the *Shacharis Amidah* at sunrise, the ideal time for that prayer

weekly parashah — The weekly Torah reading, read in shul on Shabbos morning

yahrtzeit — (Yiddish) the anniversary of a death

yasher koach — idiom expressing gratitude

yiras Shamayim — lit., *fear of Heaven;* connotes reverence for G-d, an all-pervasive attitude of piety

zechus (pl. *zechuyos*) — (n.) merit

Zeide, Zeidy —(Yiddish) grandfather; (u.c.) Grandfather

zocheh — (v.) merit

This volume is part of
THE ARTSCROLL® SERIES
an ongoing project of
translations, commentaries and expositions on
Scripture, Mishnah, Talmud, Midrash, Halachah,
liturgy, history, the classic Rabbinic writings,
biographies and thought.

For a brochure of current publications
visit your local Hebrew bookseller
or contact the publisher:

Mesorah Publications, ltd

313 Regina Avenue
Rahway, New Jersey 07065
(718) 921-9000
www.artscroll.com